ARCHAEOLOGY OF ARCHERY

First published 1991

Published by "The Glade"

British Library Cataloguing in Publication Data

A catalogue record for this book is available from the British Library.

"The Glade" ISBN 0 9517645 0 0

Dean Archaeological Group ISBN 0 9515302 1 6

Published jointly with Dean Archaeological Group.

Cover: Artist's impression, by Dave Watkins, of a Mesolithic hunting scene of some 6,000 years ago. Originally used on cover of Dean Archaeology No. 1, 1988.

ARCHAEOLOGY OF ARCHERY

by ALF WEBB

Printed in Times Roman typeface by Neolith Offset Limited, Chesham, Buckinghamshire, England

CONTENTS

List of Illustrations

The author's thanks to Roy C.Hungerford, ARPS for his superb photographs and Alain Holt, Society of Archer-Antiquaries for permission to reproduce his photograph. Thanks also to Carolyn Mortimer who supplied most of the drawings, and other members of Dean Archaeological Group for all their assistance. Special thanks to Richard Eggl for the world map.

Glossary

Archer's Paradox	The oscillation pattern of an arrow leaving the bow.
Arm	That part of a composite bow between siyah and hand grip.
Armguard	See Bracer.
Arming	The action of placing a projectile point on the arrow.
Atlati	American name for the arrow or spear-thrower.
Back	Side of the bow away from the archer when drawn.
Backing	Sinew, rawhide, etc., glued to back of bow.
Balance	Slightly off-centre mid-point of an arrow.
Braced	The bow with string in the nocks and ready to shoot. (Brace - to do so; Bracing - the act of.)
Bracing Height	The height of the string from the hand grip when the bow is braced. (See also Fistemele.)
Bow Hand	The hand holding the bow.
Cast	Maximum distance a given bow will propel an arrow; a combination of draw weight and the speed in which a bow restores to normal. Otherwise power and penetration.
Close Backed	A composite bow with a covering over the assembly of materials.
Cock feather	In a three-fletched arrow the one at right angles to the line of the nock and string. Always shot on the outside of the bow.
Composite	A bow of two or more materials.
Covering	Covering over a composite bow to keep out damp. Snake skins, leather, membrane, and notably birch bark used.
Draw	The action of pulling back the string to shoot. Sometimes refers to the method adopted to draw the arrow back. (See also Release.)
Draw Hand	The hand used to draw back the string. This hand denotes left or right-handed.
Draw length	The designed maximum length of draw.

Draw weight	The weight used to draw back the string. Always quoted as X pounds at X inches.
Ear	See Siyah.
Fistemele	Traditional measurement of bracing height. Fist with thumb upright.
Fletching	The feathers used on an arrow; the act of applying; and method of so doing.
Foreshaft	Insert in front end of an arrow; originally to carry a projectile point.
Hand grip	Point of contact of the bow hand.
Knee	Junction between siyah and arm on composite bow.
Limb	The bending portion of a bow between hand grip and bow nocks.
Loose	See Release.
Match	The arrow spine matched to cast.
Nock	The rear end of an arrow including the notch for the bow string; also string securing points on a bow
Pieced	An arrow of two or more pieces.
Prod	American term for bow portion of a crossbow.
Projectile Point	Any arrow or bolt head.
Quarrel	A four-sided crossbow bolt head.
Release	To let go the bow string.
Release aid	Any aid to drawing and releasing an arrow.
Shaft	The main portion of an arrow bearing the fletchings.
Siyah	An Arabic word meaning 'stiff, unbending'; extremity of bow limbs in composite bow.
Spine	The measurement of flexibility of an arrow.
Thumb guard	A ring or shaped piece used to protect the thumb of the bow hand when using the Mongolian release.
Thumb ring	A ring or shaped piece used to protect the thumb of the draw hand when using the Mongolian release.
Tiller	The act of securing uniform bending throughout both limb lengths.
Trajectory	Path of an arrow or bolt towards the target. Generally the greater the cast, the flatter the trajectory.

1

Introduction

Archaeologists will find it easy to classify a bow or arrow if they are fortunate enough to find them preserved. They are able to recognise and know their use because they know that similar weapons are still being used today. However, if they should find several variations in a number of weapons at one site, they will have a difficult time trying to decide whether they should take notice of the differences. They will wonder whether some of the changes in bow shape result from shrinkage, or damage, or were they made for a different purpose? They will wonder whether variously shaped arrowheads result from a preference of their makers, or were they used for a different quarry?

One cannot blame them. It is difficult to find a publication that attempts to explain the different bows, or the uses for which various arrowheads are most suited.

Sometimes the position of an artefact in the ground gives a clue as to its use. A specialised tool was found in Dynastic tombs in Nubia and explained away as a **Mace Head of Ceremonial Usage.** Unusual pieces are like sore thumbs in any archaeological collection, there is no convenient pocket name into which they can be dropped and the simple get out has often been to call them **Ceremonial** objects. A former Director of the Archaeological Survey of Nubia, proudly wrote that he had discovered their use, having found them on the thumbs of three skeletons. For the rest of his Excavation Report, he called them **Archers' Thumb Protection.** *No attempt was made to explain why tbe arcber's tbumbs needed protection.*

The skeletons of those found with archery artefacts could well tell us more about archery of the time. Fortunately there was a strong archery interest in the Mary Rose project, and cross contact between the archers and the bone specialists, produced some evidence of damage to bodies due to incorrect techniques of shooting. This has not happened elsewhere!

The human body is unlikely to show much effect from hunting, however badly the bow is handled, for at most the hunter is unlikely to be able to release more than six arrows in a full day's hunting.

But if that same archer is involved in a war situation, where the maximum number of arrows are required over the shortest possible time, incorrect techniques will quickly leave their mark on the body. Fusing of the wrist bones, and bone growth in the form of nodules on the shoulder blade are indicators to be looked for.

The majority of bow finds are of broken portions. Fortunately the type of bow often dictates where it will break and thus quite small pieces of wood can be identified as bow portions and show the type of weapon being used.

When arrows are to be considered there is considerable difficulty. An arrow can be shot from a bow - but can also be shot from a crossbow, a game trap, or thrown. A bow can shoot arrows, but can also be used to shoot what most would recognise as spears. Ethnographic parallels from those still using the bow in recent years must be considered in attempting to reconstruct the prehistoric scene.

Arrowheads are **projectile points,** but not all projectile points are arrowheads. Many can be reconstructed from drawings and photographs, but there is invariably an important detail missing from the information available. The weight of an arrowhead is rarely quoted. An arrowhead too light, or too heavy, will affect the flight of the arrow, and cause the arrow to fail to penetrate the target.

The ancillary equipment recovered can also contribute towards telling the story. Armguards - or **bracers** - start to be found in the early Bronze Age, but not much before. Why did these people suddenly need to protect their forearms? Was it a change of technique, of equipment, or of hunting demands? Were there bracers before, but were they of a material which hasn't survived the archaeological record? Or a combination of these changes?

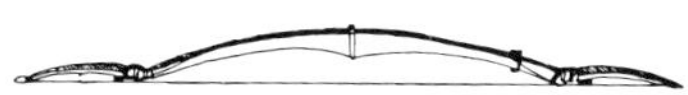

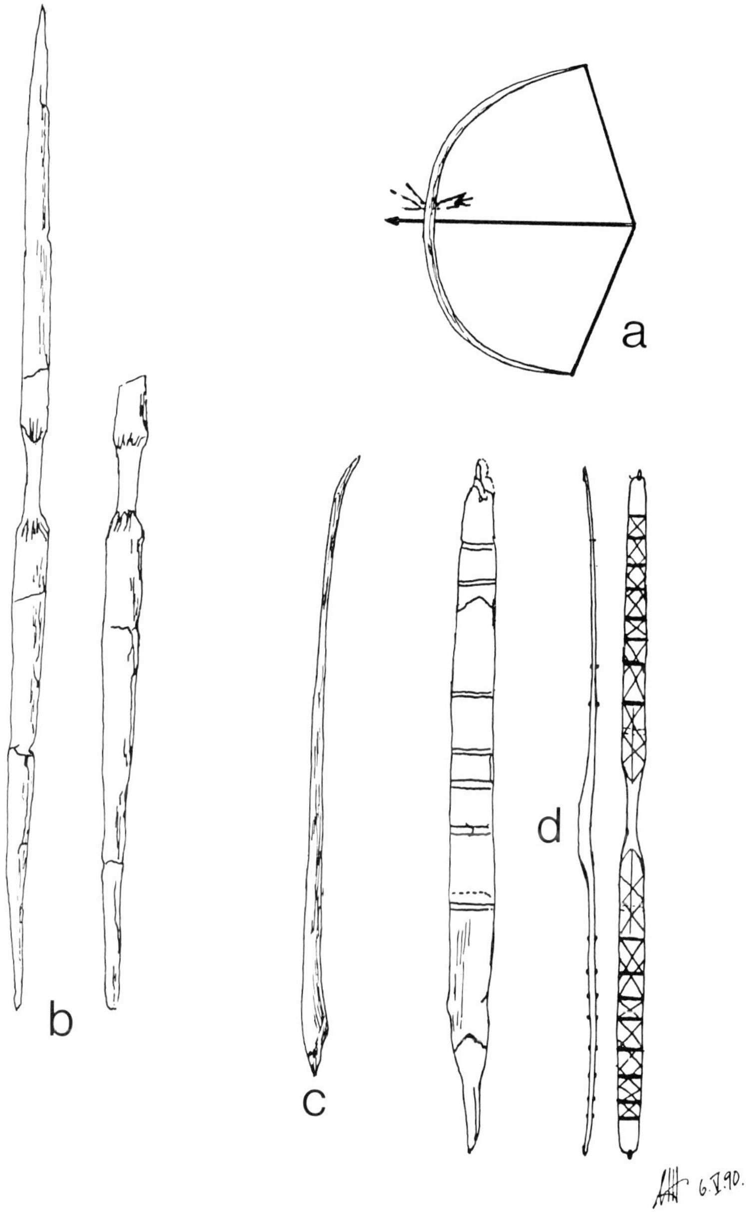

Figure 1: THE SELF BOW.
(a) The breakage point. (b) Holmgaard bow.
(c) Ashcott Heath bow. (d) Meare Heath bow and reconstruction.

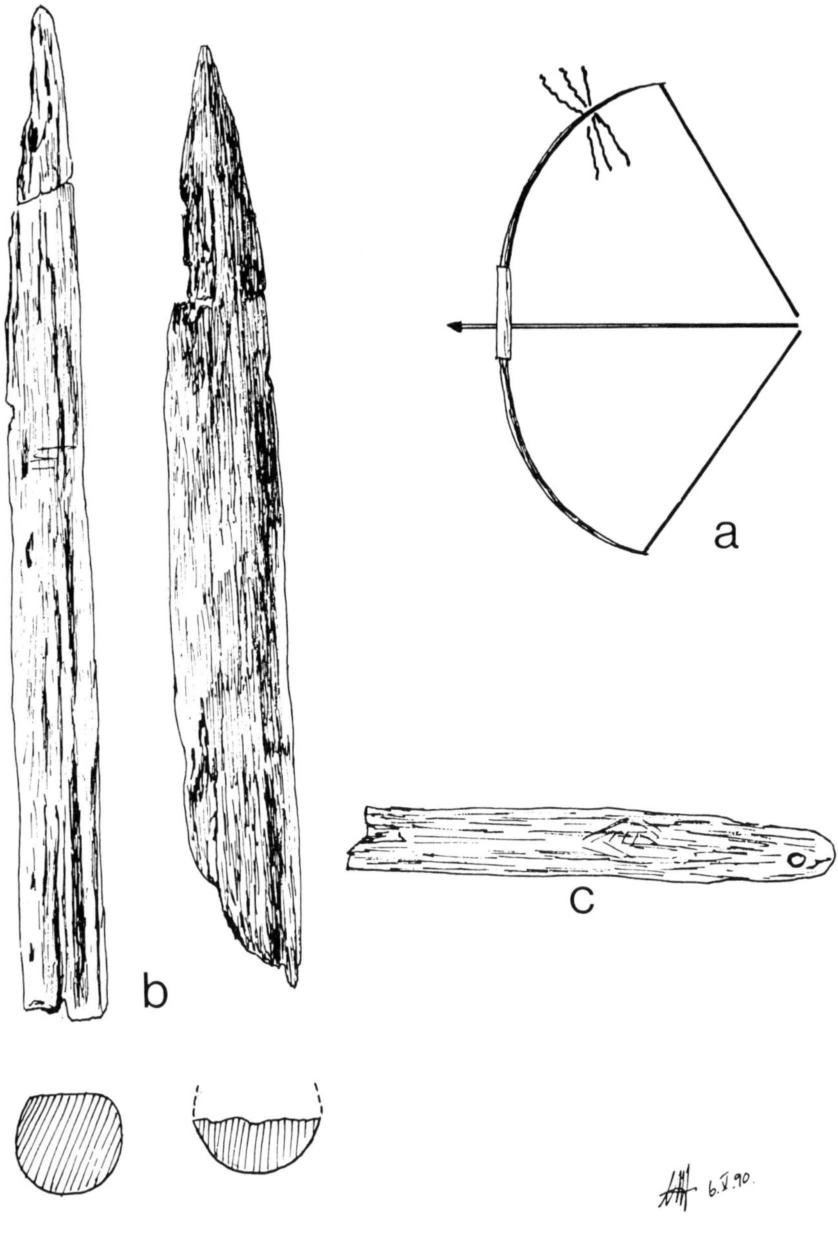

Figure 2: THE HANDLE-REINFORCED BOW.
(a) The breakage point. (b) Stellmoor Portions. (c) Drumwhinny portion.

2

Simple Bows

The **self bow** is made from one piece of timber, normally shaped by the maker before it is strung. This type of bow bends in a full arc, and is by its construction, *nine-tenths broken* every time it is drawn to the full. Such a bow should only be used for 'snap shooting,' i.e. pulled to full draw and released immediately. It will not last long if held at full draw for any length of time. Due to the full arc of the draw, these bows usually break at the point where the arrow passes **(Fig.1(a)).** The broken Holmgaard bow shows a bottom portion complete with handle, whilst the Ashcott Heath bow shows a top portion. A number of other broken bow portions of this type are known.

This simple construction is known in many native bows. Here it is usually that the wood does not last long in the climatic conditions and there is no point in spending time in making a too elaborate bow.

The **handle-reinforced bow** possibly arose because a user of a self bow felt the beginnings of a break in his hand, and decided to salvage it by binding a reinforcing piece of wood at the handle. This led to bows being made either with extra wood left on in the handle area of the bow, or, when glue became available, by glueing an extra piece of wood to the handle area. Either way, this alteration to the bowyer's art meant that the bow now bent in a restricted arc **(Fig.2(a)).** Now bows could be held at full draw, ideal for a hunter waiting the opportunity to shoot at flying game. *Probably tranchet or chisel shaped arrowheads also developed at this time. (See later Chapter.)*

These bows have a very distinctive breakage pattern. They invariably break in the upper limb, between 15 - 20 cms from the upper bow string loop. Many examples of these broken bow portions have been recovered, notably at Stellmoor. One can deduce that both types of bow remained in use for some considerable period - cave paintings in Spain clearly show both types in use at the same time.

The **long bow** is basically a handle-reinforced bow. Here the maximum material is left in the handle area, and the limbs are very gradually tapered to the bow string nocks. The art of making such a bow requires the stave to be strung right from the start, and each limb to be shaped alternatively - **tillering** - gradually increasing the draw length as more wood is removed. The final result is a very smooth arc, with the handle area non-bending, but fading into the arc so that it barely shows.

The radius of the arc centres on a point approximately one and a half times the arrow draw length **(Fig.3(a))**. The usual cross-section is **D** shaped, with the flat of the D away from the user, although it is true to say that a number are known to have been made with a rectangular cross-section.

The arrow does not pass the bow in the exact mid-point, but usually 2.5 - 3.5 cms above. The breakage pattern is not so specific as other handle-reinforced bows, but a number tend to break in the lower limb, leaving a broken portion of 45 - 60 cms in length. A bow from the Muldbjerg settlement at Aamosen, Denmark, c.3,000 BC, looks very much like a true long bow, and is broken into three parts: 35, 65 and 51 cms. A replica made of one of the Mary Rose bows, shot to destruction, also broke in the bottom limb at 51 cms. A portion of bow from Stellmoor has the D section of a long bow, and has broken at 24.8 cms - suggesting not a true long bow, but perhaps a step in the direction of one. Strangely, there is a 'fire hardened spear tip' in yew from Clacton, Essex, in D section dated some 250,000 years ago, which would be the length of a broken portion of a long bow 120 cms long.

To the uninformed a number of simple self bows look like long bows. These recovered bows are usually too fragile to be strung, so it is important that full measurements, length and cross-section, should be taken so that an interested bowyer can make a replica. Any bows broken just above the hand certainly are not long bows, they do not have the built-in handle reinforcement, and usually bend in too great an arc.

The true long bow seems to have arrived on the scene around 800 AD and became the highly esteemed war weapon of the medieval period. A number of attempts have been made to further improve the efficiency of the long bow - laminating timbers and by **pyking,** recurving the tips. (See next Chapter.)

The best timber, by far, for bows (in temperate Europe) is Yew, ***taxus baccata,*** and many bows are known in this wood. However,

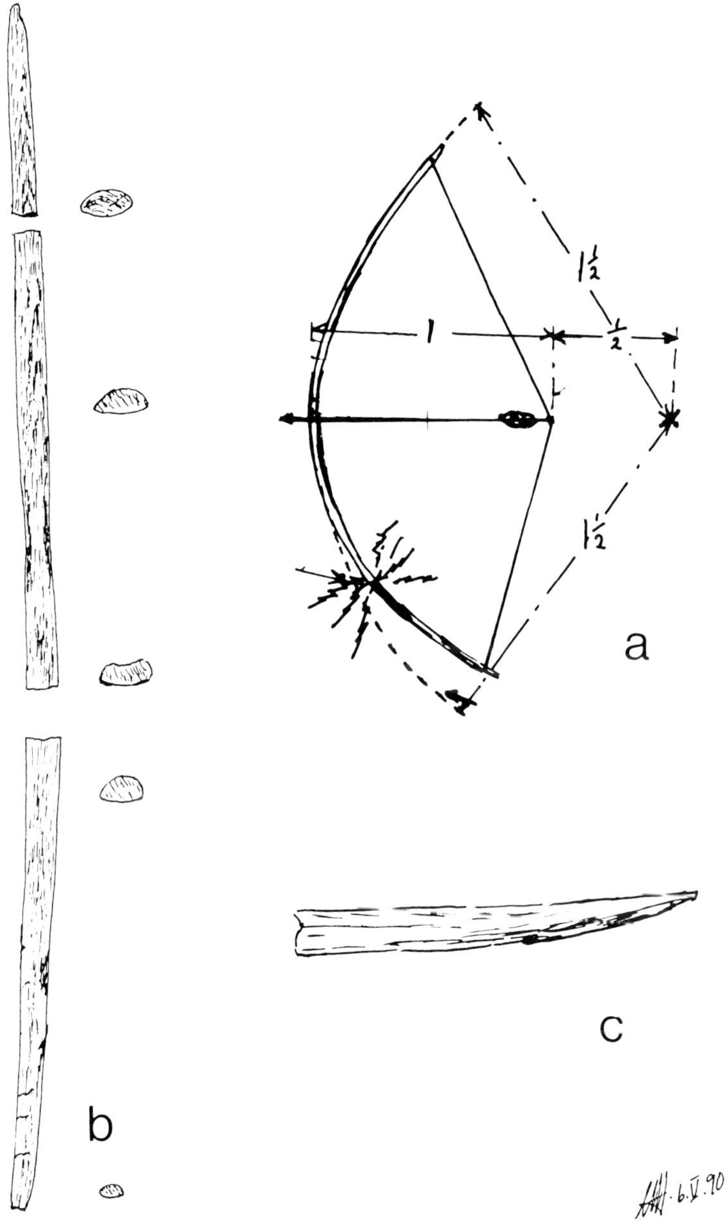

Figure 3: THE LONG BOW
(a) Proportions of a long bow. (b) Aamosen bow.
(c) Fire-hardened Spear Tip from Clacton.

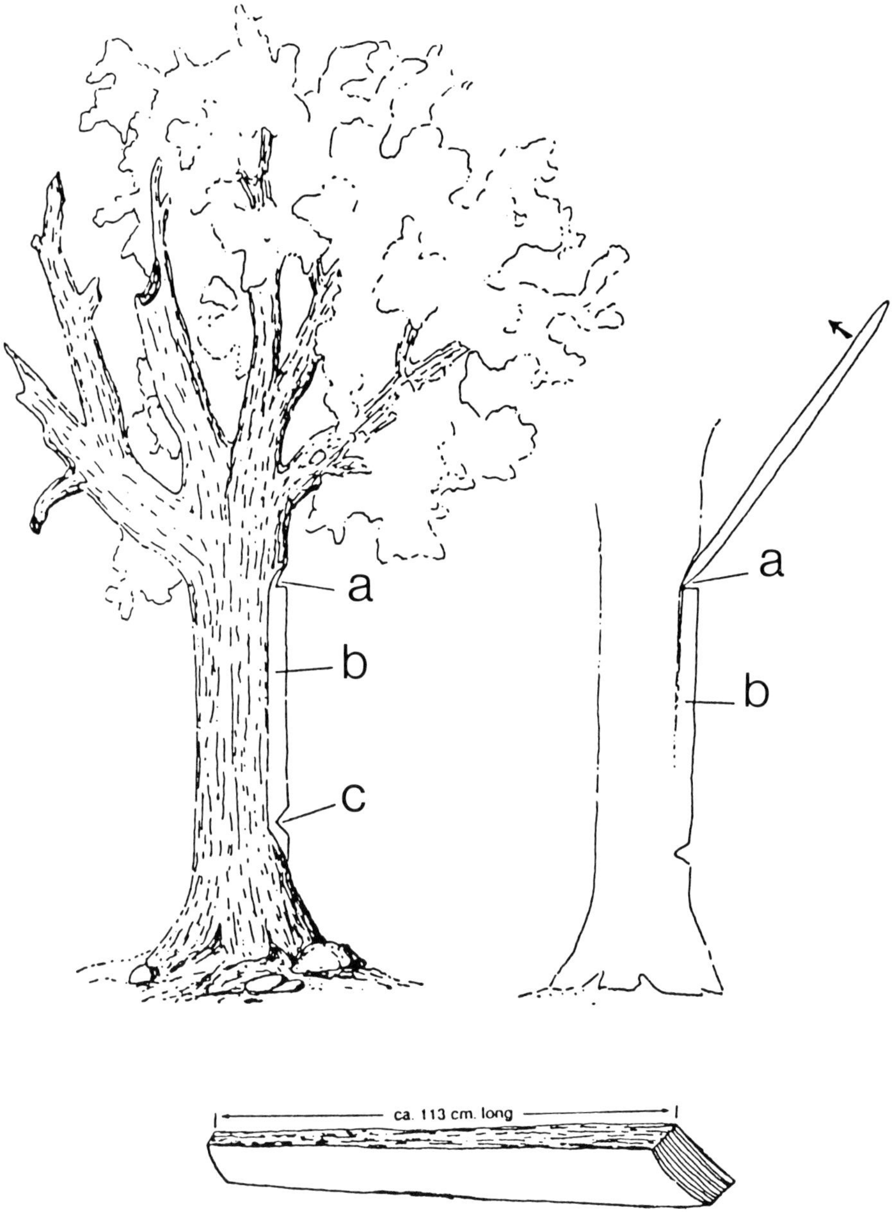

Figure 4: BOWSTAVES FROM THE LIVING TREE.
(a) Stave-removal cut. (b) Stave. (c) Growth-arrestment cut.

presumably this was not always readily available in the straight knot-free growth required, and many early bows are made from other woods -- Elm, ***ulmus,*** Oak, ***quercus,*** and Whitebeam, ***sorbus.*** There are preferred methods of seasoning the timber before it is used for bows. stacking dry, and splitting the billet over a number of years to leave both heartwood and sapwood in the same piece is the practice today, although once again ethnic parallels can suggest other methods. Finds have been made of logs in bogs. Were some logs immersed in water to season?

Philip Wilke of the University of California recently investigated a number of scarred juniper trees, ***juniperus osteosperma,*** in Western Nevada. He concluded that the Indians cut into the tree trunk at its top, made a growth arrestment cut at the bottom, and levered a stave away from the tree. This was held away from the top of the trunk for several years by a large rock or stone. He suggested that a stave 113 cms long, by 6 - 8 cms wide and 2.5 - 3 cms thick could be produced this way. **(Fig.4.)**

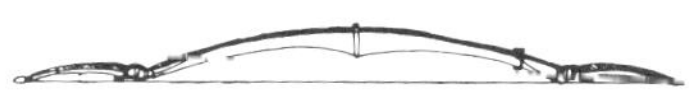

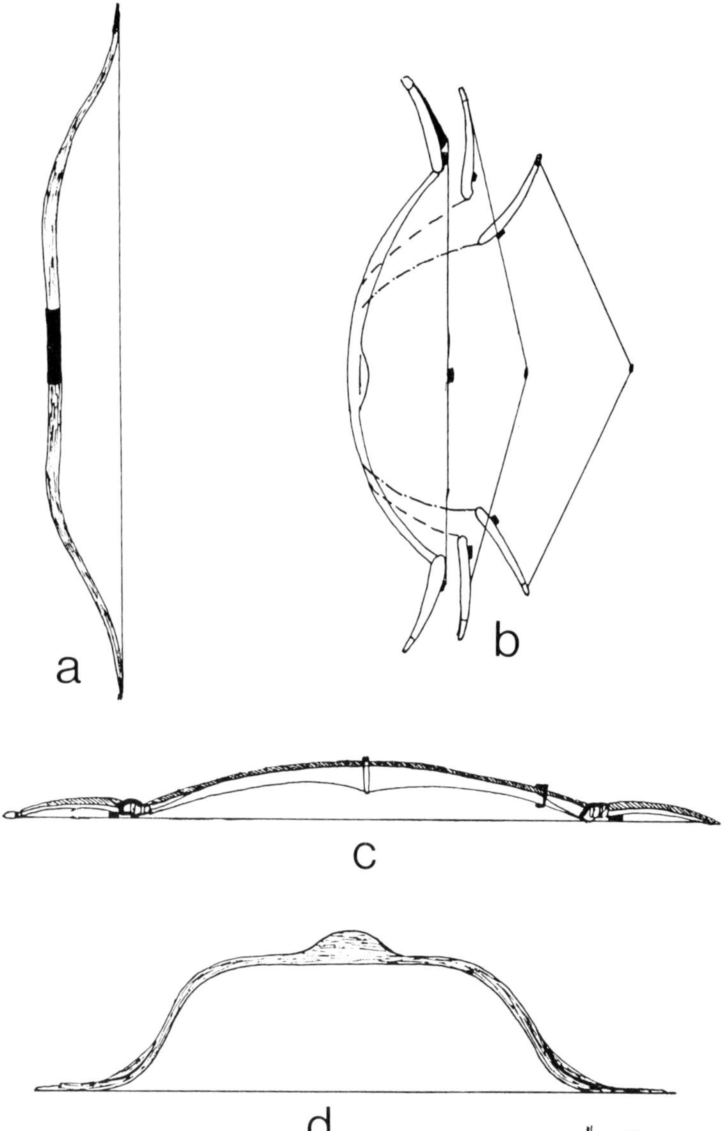

Figure 5: MORE INVOLVED BOWS.
(a) Pyked long bow. (b) Composite bow showing action of siyahs.
(c) Composite bow showing knees. (d) Close Backed Composite bow.

3

More Involved Bows

The **recurve bow** in its most simple form has the tips of the bow limbs bent back, usually under steam treatment. There is literary evidence of long bows being treated in this fashion, but evidence for steam bending has disappeared by the time the bow is recovered in an archaeological context. The two bow tips act as levers increasing the **cast** and flattens the **trajectory.** The term used in medieval documents is **pyking (Fig.5(a)).**

The **composite bow** is the term used to describe any bow that is constructed of two or more materials. The term **compound** has sometimes been used incorrectly causing some confusion to archers. They know the compound as a very late introduction, a bow with eccentric cams at the bow tips.

A reinforced composite bow has an elaborate network of sinew cables on its back to provide the cast, on a base of wood, with antler or horn belly, to provide the recovery of the bow. The **back** of a bow is that side away from the archer, the **belly** is the side nearest the archer when drawn. Even in its most primitive form a composite bow is a complex weapon - it needs a sinew back and antler or bone laths for its belly, with a high quality wooden core. It is unlikely that shortage of wood led to the composite bow, as often claimed. The core wood has to be even higher quality than that of a simple self bow. Whether one can call a bow with these materials, but not glued together, a composite - is questionable, but it may be the prototype from which true composite bows evolved when glue became available.

Tools are known by which to adjust the sinew backing to changes in humidity. It is possible that some **spatulate** tools served this purpose. Fortunately we have numbers of native bows with loose backing to study, and these can well hold the clues to the type of bow used in Palaeolithic times. It is possible that some Siberian bows may be the first steps to composite bows. Excavations by Okladnikov in the upper Angara, on the boundary of the 'Siberian-Mongolian' steppes, found shadows and parts of composite bows.

The broken bow portion from Meare Heath, Somerset, whilst being a simple self bow is strangely similar in shape to an Asiatic Composite. Was this a copy made by a bowyer who had no knowledge of the true composition of a composite bow? A wooden artefact was found during reservoir construction near the River Carron in 1889, and presented by a Mr.A.Frew to his local museum. In 1974 a report was made in **Antiquity** by Roy Switsur which claimed that this was not a paddle as originally identified but a portion of a bow. This is now called the **Denny longbow** and is displayed at Falkirk Museum. Whilst accepting these findings, we do query the bow type - the shape is reminiscent of the handle portion of a composite bow.

A distinguishing feature of many composite bows **(Fig.5(b))**, especially those with their origins in the Asiatic type, is the **Siyah,** or ear. This is a rigid extension of the bow limb, set back at an angle from the limb proper. The siyah provides leverage on the end of the bow limb, so that the bow can approach maximum draw weight earlier in the draw, thus giving a greater cast; upon release of the string, the thrust from the string diminishes at a slower rate than a bow without siyahs, and when the string reaches its point of contact with the joint of the siyah, effectively shortens the bow length, and thus further increases the cast of the bow. The joint points of bow limb to siyah are called **knees,** and there is often a bridge fitted there to prevent the bow string slipping past when braced or shot.

Another type of composite bow is so well finished as to seem to uninformed eyes to be of one piece construction. This is the **close backed** bow - usually a core of wood is backed by sinew and faced with horn, but the whole is covered in skin or leather. These type of composites could have found their way into Britain with the Roman forces. Ronald Embleton has produced a superb reconstruction painting based on information supplied by Russell Robinson of an Hamian archer, ***cohors Hamiorum Sagittariorum,*** on a tomb stone from Housesteads. There is a report of a 'recurved horn bow' being found in the Cambridgeshire Fens between Waterbeach and Ely in 1856. Where it is now, if it still exists, is unknown.

Hamilton suggests that the basic principles of the composite bow were apparently worked out independently in North America more or less simultaneously with the advent of the horse on the Western Plains around 1700. The American version dispenses entirely with wood; the sinew back is glued directly to the horn belly.

There is no regular breakage pattern with the composite bow. Many would have limbs break, but these would be fairly easy to replace. The broken limbs would be difficult to identify. The only portion likely to be recognised would be the handle portion, with probably the upper and lower limb attachment points badly worn.

NOTES

4

Bowstrings

Bowstrings have been, and are made of a great variety of materials. Some of the earliest, no doubt, would have been animal tendons, probably from the rear legs of large quadrupeds to obtain the length required. Two bows from the collection in King Tut'ankhamun's tomb retain scraps of gut string, which has melted into a viscid mass. Animal sinew, however, fluctuates in length according to the prevailing humidity and would need constant adjustment to obtain the optimum **bracing height** of the bow. The bracing height of a bow measured in the old fashioned way is one **fistemele**, the height of the fist with thumb upright, an average of 15 - 17 cms. Too low and the string administers a very sharp thwack on the lower wrist - too high, the upper forearm gets hit. A number of bows are known with holes in their upper limbs to allow quick adjustments to be made. Desmond Castle, Drumwhinny and Ballinderry Crannog are examples.

All sorts of vegetable fibre have been used. Lime and willow make good bast fibres capable of being worked into thread. Elsewhere ramie and china grass have been used. Flax, ***linum usitatissimon,*** from whence the word **Linen** is given to the thread obtained from its fibres, is one of the strongest natural fibres known. Many bowstrings have been made of this.

Godwin shows a pollen curve for Hemp, ***cannabis sativa,*** from East Anglia spanning a period in excess of 3,000 years. Good hemp bowstrings ***(nervis)*** were always recorded as the 'best' strings in the medieval period - purchasers were warned of adulterants, particularly the common hemp nettle, ***galeopsis tetrahit,*** being used to bulk out the hemp.

C.sativa originated in Western Asia and seems to have been cultivated there for both its fibre and for its narcotic properties for over a thousand years BC. The cultivation spread into the Middle East, through ancient Scythia, and by AD 100 was being grown commercially in Sicily and Italy. **Lucilius** mentions it c.100 BC., and later both **Pliny** and **Cato** wrote about it. It had reached Scandinavia by AD 800 as seeds of the plant were found in bedding materials in the Viking ship-burial at Oseberg.

Silk is another substance used. The coarse varieties of wild silk can be spun like cotton to produce thread - many early bowstrings of this material were treated with glue. A strip of bamboo is used for bowstrings in many parts of the world. *Museum curators with bamboo strung bows might like to note that the inner side of the bamboo strip should face the belly of the bow. If bent the other way it breaks.*

It is not really good practice to leave a bow on display with its string in the braced position. If the string breaks considerable damage can be done to the bow and other objects in the display case. Often as not, one will see bows braced backwards, for many composite bows are reflex, i.e. the bow limbs curve or sweep backwards from the grip when the bow is relaxed. They are originally made in this way, and as the sinew backing dries it contracts the limbs further back into the reflex position. It just seems right to join those two reflexed bow tips with a string. One small draw on the string in this position certainly means a broken bow.

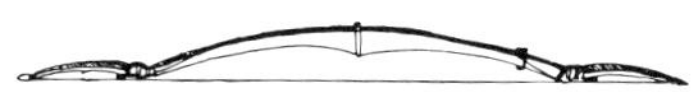

5

Arrows

The report by Prof. Pratt and Robert Hardy on *"The Arrow Found in Westminster Abbey in 1878,"* is a model of the type of information required by those wishing to replicate finds of arrows. They give the total weight of the arrow (42.6g), make an informed estimate of the weight of the shaft alone (36.6 - 39.6g) and from this, knowing the volume of the shaft calculate the density of the wood (0.57 - 0.62 x 10^3 kg/m^3). They then determined the elastic stiffness of the wood and the archers' **spine** measurement. From standard tables of wood density, the species of wood was able to be considered, and deductions made as to the **draw weight** of the bow likely to have been used.

The amount of information that can be obtained from one arrow properly investigated may cause some surprise to archaeologists. In order to show why such information is important, let us consider some points on the use of arrows.

The first consideration in choosing an arrow to shoot from a bow is that it is **matched.** This is so that the full **archers' paradox** is possible **(Fig.6(a)).** An arrow with its **spine** matched to the **cast** will not actually touch the bow from the moment the string is **released.** The initial impact of the released string on the arrow bends it toward and then away from the side of the bow. This oscillation continues during the time the string is pushing forward. Finally, if the oscillation period is just right, the tail end of the arrow curves around the bow, its fletchings nicely clearing all obstacles. Once clear of the bow and free of the string, the arrow rights itself by springing back to bend in the reverse plane and continues in a series of diminished oscillations until it is flying on its original and intended course.

If an arrow is too stiff, it strikes the bow somewhere during the release, causing scattering to the left (in a right handed archer). Not only that, it also makes a noise thus warning the quarry. If an arrow has been made too thin and too flexible, it also strikes the bow, but

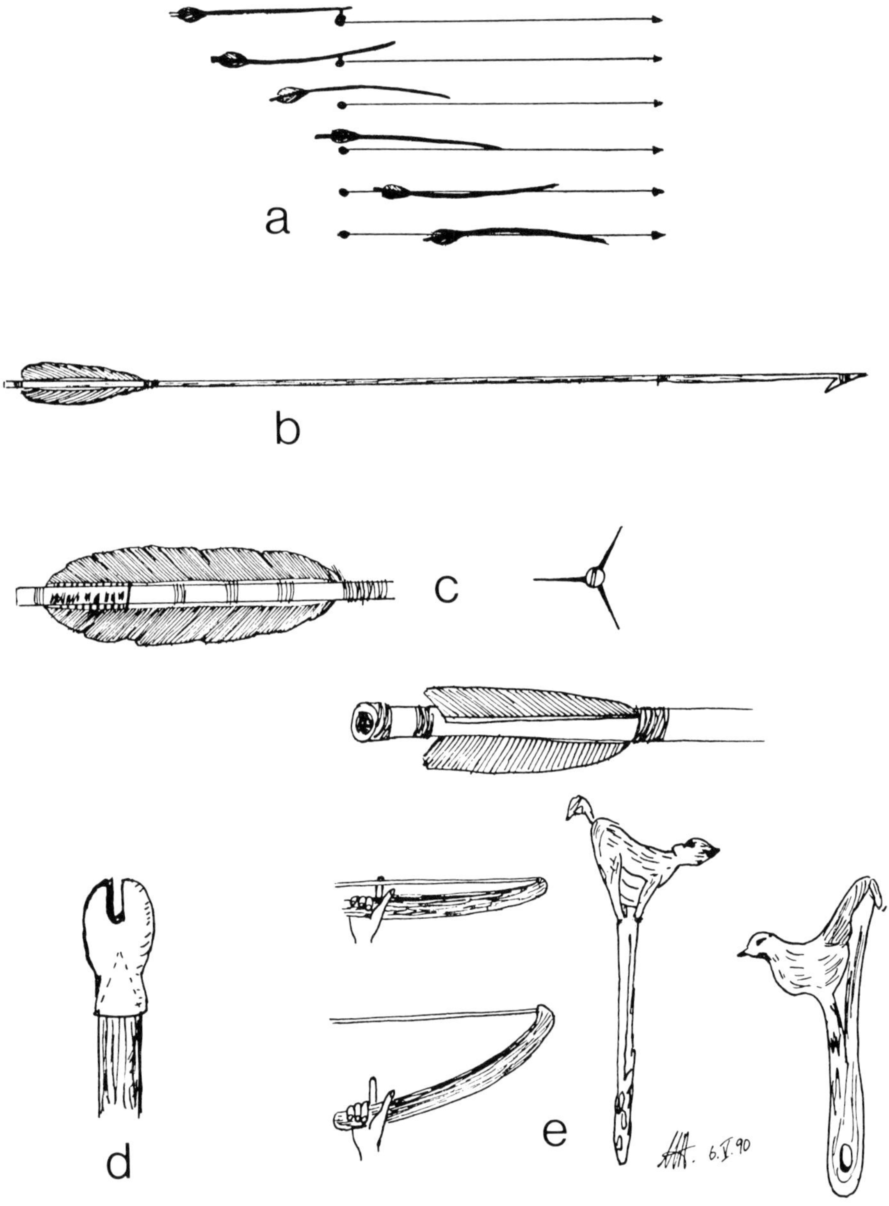

Figure 6: ARROWS.
(a) Archer's Paradox. (b) Pieced Arrow. (c) Fletching. (d) Bulbous Nock.
(e) Cupped nock. Examples of Throwers and method of use.

very often the degree of bending it receives from the release will cause it to break. Some very nasty injuries have occurred due to arrows breaking in the bow, especially when the fracture of an arrow has not been noticed and it is shot again. One method of overcoming this problem is to use **pieced** arrows **(Fig.6(b))**.

These are known from many lands. The **foreshaft** containing the arrowhead on a short section of thin shaft, is inserted into the longer main shaft, which can be stiffer to overcome the paradox problem. These arrows have advantages. When a hit is made, and the animal flees, the main shaft can drop out and indicate a hit. The short foreshaft portion is difficult to dislodge by rubbing against undergrowth. A further advantage is that not so many main shafts need to be carried, a very important consideration when the hunter is on foot and covering a large territory.

The pieced arrow overcomes another problem. When an arrow shaft is split or notched to receive a projectile point, the diameter of the shaft places a definite limit on the thickness of the arrowhead which can be wedged into the split or notch. A larger projectile point can be fitted into a split or notch of a foreshaft thicker than the main shaft and, providing that the balance of the arrow is kept (by heavier fletchings, or heavier nock) and the cast of the bow is there, will still work well. It is how the projectile point is mounted that determines its weight.

The second consideration is the length of the arrow. When an archer is pulling the bow to draw the arrow to its head, then it has to be of a length naturally encompassed by the user's arms. This means that most arrows are from 70 - 90 cms long. However there are instances where arrows can be twice or more this length (which we will come to later).

Fletchings, or the feather flighting of arrows, are not always necessary. They do not have much effect on guiding an arrow until it is completely past the aforementioned paradox, say 25 - 30 metres. Thus many peoples do use unfletched arrows as their skills allow them to approach their quarry to closer distances. On the other hand most of the extra length arrows are not found fletched. The extra length of shaft gives the **balance** to the arrow in the same way as fletchings. Even in communities where 'normal' length fletched arrows are in common use, fishing is carried out with extra length arrows. The constant immersion in water soon makes fletchings useless, and the extra length of arrow is handier to reach to pull fish out of the water.

Where ever fletchings are used, although the method of securing to the shaft will differ considerably, most tend to use three feathers. One, the **cock** feather is placed at right angles to the slot in the **nock,** the other two placed equidistant around the shaft so that there are 120 degrees between all three **(Fig.6(c)).** The arrow is always shot with the cock feather away from the bow. *It is incorrect to term the other feathers **hen** feathers.* All three feathers have to be from one wing - normally the right wing feathers only are used (for a right-handed archer).

The **balance** of the arrow is another important factor. The centre of balance should be just forward of the mid-point of the arrow, otherwise the arrow will not fly horizontally. This can obviously be affected by the size and weight of the arrowhead, and can be offset in some instances by using longer and larger fletchings, and heavier **nocks.** The bronze nocks on arrows from Hedeby, Schleswig Holstein would have helped to counter balance the heavy iron arrowheads used.

Nocks, that portion of an arrow that fits on the bowstring are another consideration where there is immense variety. The straight forward slot in the arrow, possibly bound to avoid splitting of the arrow, is the most common. Other arrows can be found with a completely flattened end. These can be either arrows shot from a crossbow, or arrows shot by archers whose techniques involve holding the arrow to the string with the fingers. Other arrows can be found where the cut nock is reinforced by extra wood, bone or antler, making a bulbous nock **(Fig.6(d))**. These are most likely to be used in composite bows with a thumb-release method of shooting.

One other type of nock, which involves a cup-like cavity in the end of the arrow, is a certain indicator that the arrow was made for throwing, with a spear-thrower, rather than being shot from a bow. American archaeologists consider that the first people to enter their continent carried spear-throwers as their main weapon. It is called an **atlati** in America. In Europe too, the Magdalenians certainly had these spear-throwers. They made notched batons with a point at one end which engaged in the hollow cup-like depression in the arrow or spear at the nock end.

The shaft of the arrow, or spear, was laid along the top of the baton, with its end engaged in the cup, and the whole cast with an overhand swing, retaining the baton in the hand. Since the length of the thrower's arm was increased by the length of the baton, plus an added leverage effect, the technique propelled an arrow or spear a considerable distance **(Fig.6(e)).** There are indications that the spear-thrower pre-dates the bow - in Australia the thrower is used throughout. A little evidence of the bow exists in territory close to Papua/ New Guinea, but this died out when the deep sea channel was formed.

Arrows are made from a wide variety of materials. Where bamboo cane or reeds of the necessary strength are available, these are used. Wood is used in Northern Europe - shafts from Stellmoor, Loshult and Vinkelmose for example, were made from pine, ***pinus,*** and from other sites arrows have been recovered made from hazel, ***corylus,*** and the Guelder rose, ***viburnam opulus***.. Blunt wooden arrowheads used to stun small birds and game, when made complete with the arrow or as separate heads, have been found made from birch, ***betula***..

Our greatest source of medieval arrows, the Mary Rose project, finds most arrows made from aspen poplar, ***populus tremula.*** Roger Ascham, *Toxophilus: the Schole or Partitions of Shooting,* 1545, would have considered these arrows inferior. He listed birch, ***betula,*** hornbeam, ***carpinus,*** some oak, ***quercus,*** some ash, ***fraxinus,*** being both strong enough to stand in a bow, but also light enough to fly. He also said: *"yet as concerning sheaths of arrows for war it were better to make them out of good ash and not of aspen* ***as they are nowadays."***

NOTES

6

Arrowheads

Every arrowhead is a projectile point but every projectile point is not necessarily an arrowhead.

That very important statement being reiterated, it is perhaps understandable that it is difficult to identify the first arrowheads. Assuming the microliths of the Mesolithic period are the first attempts at arrowheads, let us consider how they could have been used. An arrow from Loshult is often used to illustrate how microliths could have been used to arm an arrow. The recovered arrow had two microliths secured to it - one as a point and one further back. There are other ways these microliths could have been used.

Ethnographic evidence from Africa, for example, demonstrates two other ways. Allchin illustrates a Bushman arrow where poison was placed on the worked edges of the flint, which was then buried in gum mastic at the point of the arrow, making in effect a barbed arrowhead **(Fig.7(a)).** Once this head entered the quarry, the gum melted, released the poisoned flints and allowed the poison to enter the quarry's bloodstream. Nearby in the Mjobo reserve, bowmen were found using just the sharpened wooden points of arrows as arrowheads, but they had placed three geometrically shaped flints around the shaft like miniature fletchings some 5 cms back from the point **(Fig.7(b)).** The theory here being that the flints provided a stop-ridge and prevented the arrow penetrating deeper into the quarry, and keeping the poison to the outer skin.

Both these methods required poison to be released into the animal's bloodstream. There is apparently no evidence at present that poison was being used in archery in Northern Europe in the Mesolithic period, although there is evidence of enough plants producing poison being available. The common spurge, ***euphorbia,*** is widespread in Britain - the smallest dose of the sap from this plant will put fish and

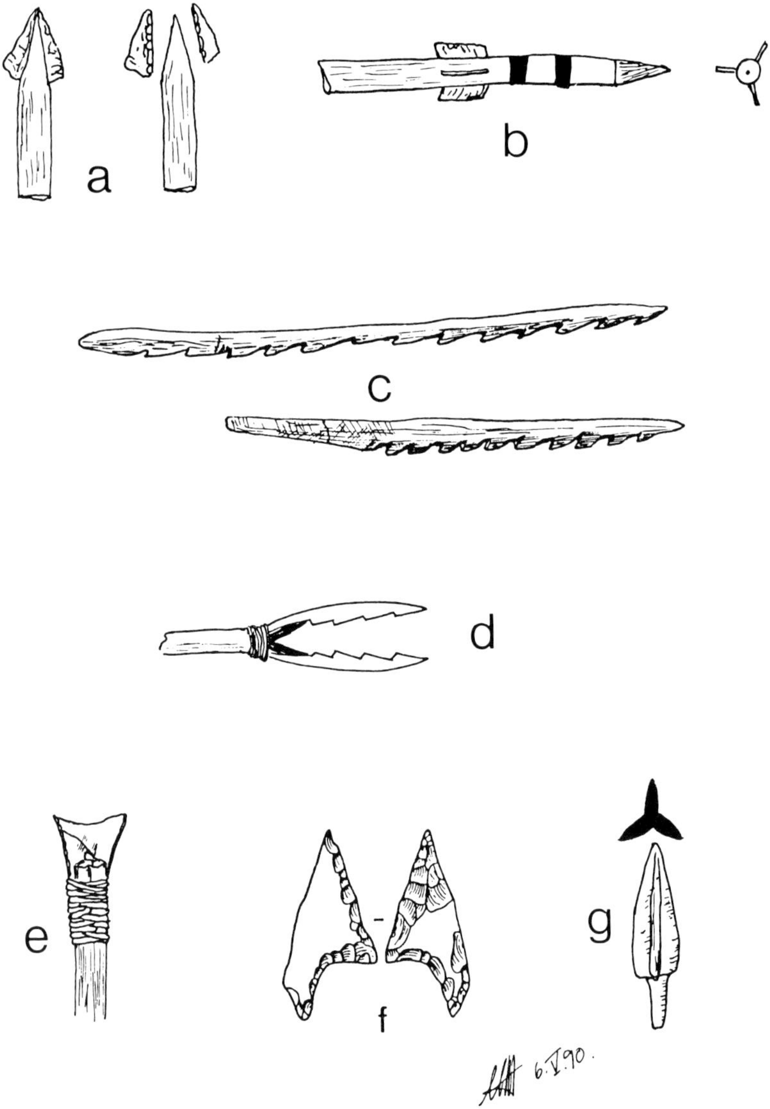

Figure 7: ARROWHEADS.
(a) Bushmen arrowhead. (b) Mjobo arrowhead. (c) Harpoons. (d) Leister.
(e) Tranchet arrowhead. (f) Fengate arrowhead. (g) Roman/Scythian type arrowhead.

animals quickly to sleep - a fact well-known to the 'travelling folk' for centuries. From experience with early replica bows, I believe that it is possible that poison was being used. The microliths do not produce a life-threatening wound and the bows do not appear to have a great penetrative power.

Harpoons are known from very early times. Clark illustrates "points more or less cylindrical in section symmetrically tapered at either end and slotted on one or both edges. No example has yet been found hafted, but being pointed at either end looks as though they were intended to fit into a socket in the forepart of a shaft and traces of resin used to set them more firmly frequently appears at one end." **(Fig.7(c)).** He goes on to question whether they were propelled by bows or throwers. From Heath and Chiara, one learns that the Brazilian Indians use the bow at all times to shoot larger fish in deep waters, and when rivers and lakes flood in the wet season, the Indians rely on boat-fishing with the bow and arrow. As with many other communities poisoning the water to semi-stun the fish is often practised. Canoes are used when large fish are pursued, and barbed or serrated harpoon headed arrows must be used, otherwise the movements of the struggling fish will dislodge the arrow.

In Brazil the barbed hardwood arrowheads or harpoons are inserted into the arrowshafts in multiple arrangements with barbs inward or outward facing in the form of a **leister (Fig.7(d)).** They have long tapering tangs into the foreshaft and the exposed portion can measure up to 50 cms in length. The complete arrows are necessarily extra length to provide balance. In Melanesia, the heads are of bamboo, but here three or more barbed points are carved from the one bamboo, the rear ends not separated from the bamboo, and bound so that they spread out. Before shooting the tips are lightly tied together, making one point, and as the head enters the fish, the tie gives and the barbed points spring out to hold the fish.

As suggested in Chapter 2, tranchet or chisel-shaped arrowheads seem to go naturally with the handle-reinforced bow **(Fig.7(e)).** Whilst it is fairly easy to join a group with shot-guns shooting at almost tame partridge and pheasant, there is absolutely no opportunity to shoot at birds with the bow in the United Kingdom. Such shooting has to be restricted to other wilder, less civilised countries with consequent problems. Usually such expeditions require considerable funds to get there and once there time is limited and one can only shoot for the pot. (Otherwise one is no better than the 'big game hunters' of past years, just notching up a bag.)

The archer having volunteered to shoot for the pot, in order to feed the rest of the party, finds it takes time to learn the techniques. One certainly needs a bow that can be held comfortably at near full draw for long periods. Ordinary broadheads, as used on other game, have very little effect on flying game if the body is missed. They seem to be able to pass through wing feathers without causing damage. The tranchet-shaped arrowheads do, however tend to cut quills, causing loss of flying ability and the grounded birds can be quickly despatched. In the Kalahari desert, one of the groups of San, the **G/We,** sometimes make arrows double-ended, i.e. nocked at both ends, with ostrich shell fletchings at both ends. When shot, these turn end over end in the air and can bring down quite large birds.

Distinctive arrowheads appear in the Neolithic period in Britain: the leaf shape, a general purpose hunting head, and the tranchet which I suggest were for flying game. At Fengate, Peterborough, a number of arrowheads were recovered. They appeared to be barbed and tanged with one barb broken off, and also were made on a curve, instead of the normal flat section. They intrigued me! I do apologise to the Director of Excavations, I was more interested in those arrowheads than what he was saying.

When I got home I made some replicas and tried shooting them. Using a sight, they tended to drop about 30 cms below similar groups using replica fully barbed arrows. Shooting in an instinctive style, without fixed sights, they dropped short. Then I tried shooting them at weighted washing-up bottles floating at various depths in a pool, and gained a good proportion of hits. The 'lop-sided' weighting seemed to counter-act the water parallax, and led me to believe they were designed purely for fishing. I am aware of 'micro wear studies,' where wear patterns on flint edges are studied, but can these studies show a difference between an arrowhead used to cut animal flesh and one used purely on fish?

The barbed and tanged arrowheads of the Beaker folk are without doubt some of the finest ever produced. They are the 'archer's arrowhead,' and every time one is recovered from a field walking expedition, I still experience that thrill of finding the perfect arrowhead.

Another group of arrowheads, mainly recovered from Cornwall, Devon and South Wales - Bronze Age 2000 - 1400 BC - are very large finely flaked triangular types. Usually 3.7 - 4 cms long, and nearly as wide, they are much bigger and heavier than the Beaker arrowheads. Often they are of a dark flint, almost slate-like in appearance and many are extremely thin. In fact so thin, that I wonder if they would stand up to being shot from a bow. Could it be that they were not used in the bow? Could it be that they were being used as currency or authority? There is ethnographical precedence for arrowheads to be used as currency.

There is a little evidence for the use of the bow in the Iron Age, it certainly did not seem to hold the same importance as it did in early time. Tanged arrowheads of iron dating from the First Century BC have been found, but far more baked clay and stone sling stones. Some La Tene burials have still had flint arrowheads buried with them. Whether there is an equation - iron arrowheads = war, flint arrowheads = hunting, I would not know.

The Roman invasion brought fresh arrowheads into the country. Triangular sectioned bronze and iron arrowheads of a Scythian type have been recovered from Roman sites **(Fig.7(g))**. The bow used with these arrows would have been the composite.

Hazelwood arrows with iron arrowheads have been found from the Saxon period, as has one bow. Flint continued to be used in native equipment for many centuries. So-called 'Irish' arrowheads of around AD 800 - 900 have been recovered along the Peddar's Way. Some Viking equipment has been recovered, but little from the early medieval period.

By the 13th Century, it would seem that manufacture was concentrated on **quarrels** (Heads for crossbow bolts) - over a million were made at St. Briavels in the Forest of Dean. Military manufacture of arrowheads does not appear in the records until early in the 14th Century - just prior to the Battle of Crecy.

For arrowheads of this time, the London Museum catalogue is without parallel, but it does not differentiate between heads for arrows or for crossbow bolts. It is hoped that further research and excavation at St. Briavels will enable a listing of quarrel types for the period AD 1200 - 1300 to be made.

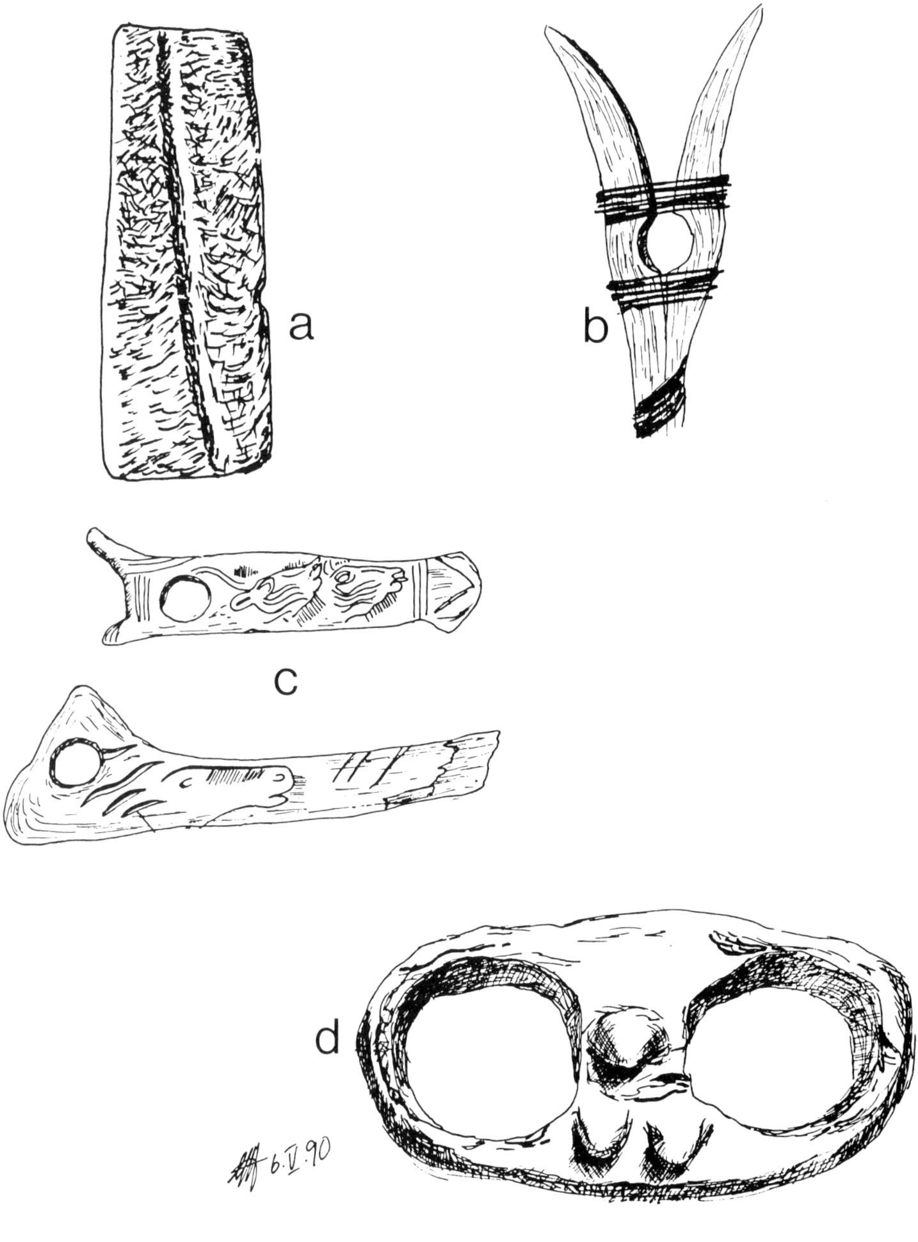

Figure 8: ANCILLARY EQUIPMENT.
(a) Arrow Shaft Smoother. (b) Arrow Straightener.
(c) Batons de Commandement. (d) Bogenspanner.

7

Ancillary Equipment

Arrow Shaft Smoothers are usually of a coarse gritty sandstone, in pairs, with a groove in each. These would be placed either side of the shaft and rubbed up and down **(Fig.8(a))**.

Arrow Straighteners can be recognised. Often **Y** shaped bone with an enlarged hole at the joint of the Y, they would be used in the same way as an electrician bends conduit **(Fig.8(b))**. The one illustrated by Evans has been used by some to incorrectly suggest the use of the next artefact.

Batons de Commandement have often been suggested as arrow straighteners. Generally the holes are too large to be effective for the diameter of the arrows used **(Fig.8(c))**.

Bearing Arrows are arrows made as 'Wands of Office' to denote the bearer's authority. Usually they are larger, or thicker and heavier than shootable arrows, and often the heads are in a different material to the norm.

Bogenspanner is the name attached to artefacts found in Etruscan Sites. They consist of a double ring, mostly in bronze, with vertical Spikes - usually three - on one side. They have been identified by some as 'bow pullers,' and many have attempted to discuss this identification. They have been alternatively identified as: calthrops or tribulus; spear-throwers; snaffle curbs or bits; lamp wick holders; for preventing a load slipping; for helping a driver grasp reins; an early form of knuckle-duster and religious amulets. **(Fig.8(d))** shows one.

I believe that they are connected with divination and bear a strong resemblence to models of lambs livers. These models replaced the freshly killed liver used in ceremonies to predict the future health of patients. the **Piancenza Bronze** from Italy has these three spikes, and the whole of the body of the object is bisected by lines with engraved instructions in each segment which tell the Shaman, or priest, what answer to give. The usual method of using these objects is to hold them between a thumb and fore finger, to throw a straw or hair into the air and catch it with the object. The position the straw or hair takes will lie across one of the marked segments and give the answer required.

Bracers, or Armguards, begin to appear in the archaeological record in the early Bronze Age. Whether they were in use before, but were made of a material which has not survived, or whether they were a new introduction, cannot be decided. There is one point worth making. Anybody who has tried shooting a bow for the first time invariably receives a bruised forearm in the process. This is normally because the bow has been held too long - the longer a bow is held at full draw, the more apt one is to hit the arm. Let us consider the bracer as a new introduction. The archer now has the handle-reinforced bow and tranchet tipped arrows shooting at flying game. The optimum hunting style for this requires the bow to be held at almost full draw, the birds to be beaten by helpers towards the bows, and arrows to be released as the birds pass over. The bracer would now be required. **(Fig.9(a))** shows a selection of bracers.

There is another type of bracer which really ought to be called a 'Thumb Guard.' Used with the Mongolian release (see later Chapter) it covers the thumb of the bow hand preventing damage as the arrow is drawn past it. The 'Nubian Treasure' excavator (mentioned in the Introduction) reported on several finds. They were cut from a piece of sheet silver and bent to fit the hand. Silver rivets on the thumbpiece were used to attach the chain which passed round the thumb of the user, and two holes were bored at the end of the wings, probably for a leather thong for attachment to the wrist. All had engraved decoration **(Fig.9(b))**.

Charcoal and other colouring material. Many Mesolithic sites have produced finds of charcoal and ochre. Usually these are reported as aids to personal decoration but it is worth pointing out ethnographical evidence where these colours were used to symbolically mark arrows: black for death; red for blood, etcetra.

Chelik is the name given to a thin piece of ivory or horn set across the grip of a composite bow, so that two pieces of horn forming the belly, butt on to it. Often highly decorated.

Gorytus is the name given to the combined quiver and bowcase used by many with the composite bow. These cases were carried by mounted archers, and one would have expected them to be in use

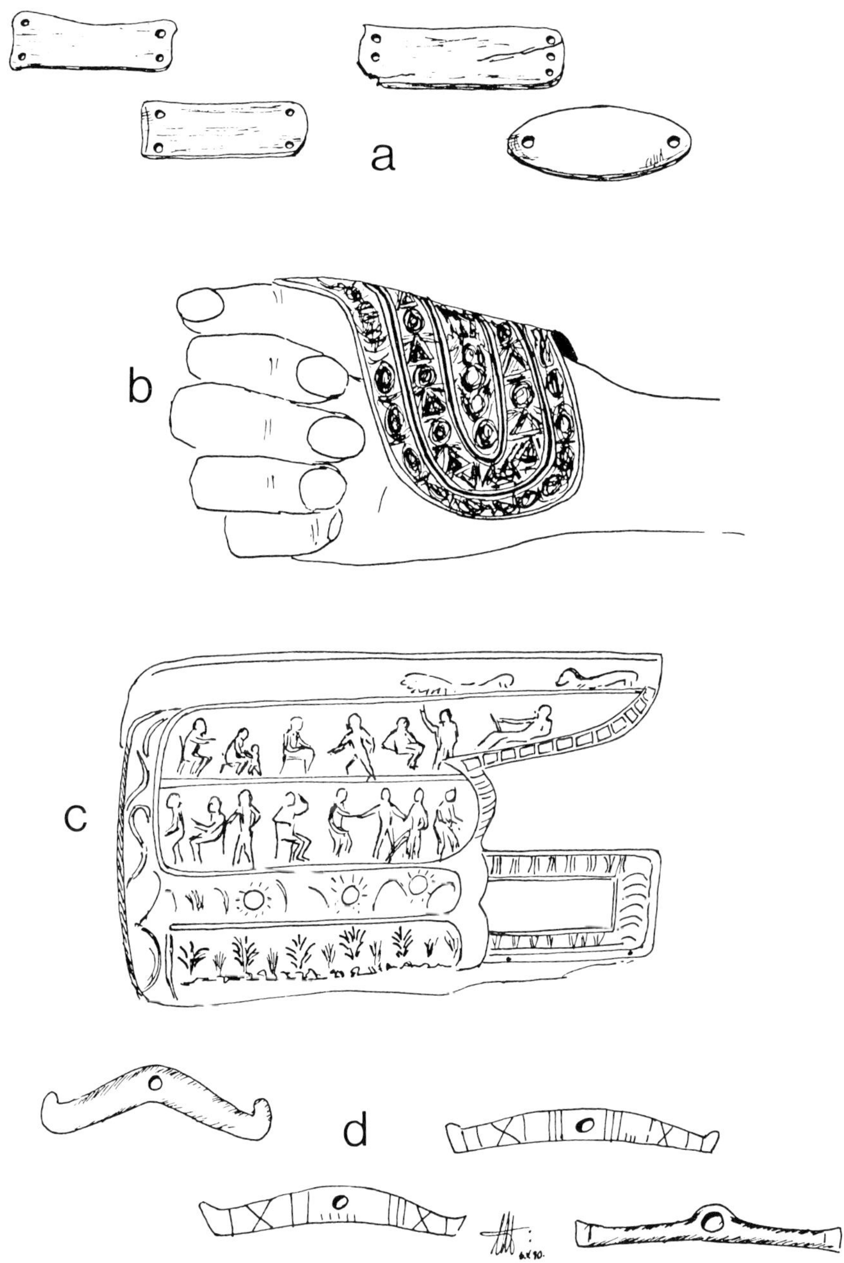

Figure 9: ANCILLARY EQUIPMENT.
(a) Selection of Bracers. (b) Thumb Guard. (c) Gorytus. (d) Pendants.

among those auxiliary archers used by the Romans in Britain **(Fig.9(C)).**

Pellet Bow is a variety of bow adapted for shooting stones or clay balls. When this bow was first known in Europe cannot be decided, but it certainly had its uses in wild fowling. An early reference appears in Rymer's **Feodera** in that in 1327, citizens of London were being disturbed by hooligans armed with **ballistas et arcus pro lapidis** from which they shot **lapides ac pelotes tereas.** The bows resemble an ordinary long bow except that the hand grip is set below centre, and the string divides half-way down to accommodate a small disc against which the pellet is held.

Henry VIII knew the pellet bow and when he died in 1547, an inventory was made of the armoury at Westminster which contained **two longe bowes of Ewghe to shote stones in with cases of Lether to them.**

Pendants are found in male Bronze Age burials. These are often shaped like a bow with markings that could be interpreted as bindings for a composite bow. They show 'ears' and in the centre of the crescent shape, a hole. Piggott made the suggestion that they were indeed replicas of composite bows **(Fig.9(d)).** Another suggestion (Frey, 1990), has been made and will be discussed under 'Release Aids.'

Poles. It is noted that in some parts of the world, a pointed pole is also part of the archer's equipment. These have a dual use. The pole is used to support and steady the bow hand, and is also used as a secondary defence when the first arrow shot fails to kill. This is not to be confused with the stakes used by archers at Agincourt to protect their lines against cavalry charges. In later medieval times several writers suggested incorporating the bow with the pike. In Lapland, both bow and pole could be found fitted with basket and spike in the form of ski sticks for travel in snow.

Quivers are the carrying cases for arrows. They can be free-standing alongside the user or they can be worn. As far as is known, none have been recovered in an archaeological context in Northern Europe, but one cannot say they were not used. Bronze Age burials have produced quantities of arrowheads ranged so neatly together that they must have been either placed in a quiver or tied in a bundle before burial. Quivers were in use in prehistoric times - two were found in King Tut'ankhamun's tomb (1361 - 1352 BC). On the Bayeux tapestry large wooden quivers can be seen stood on the ground by the archers.

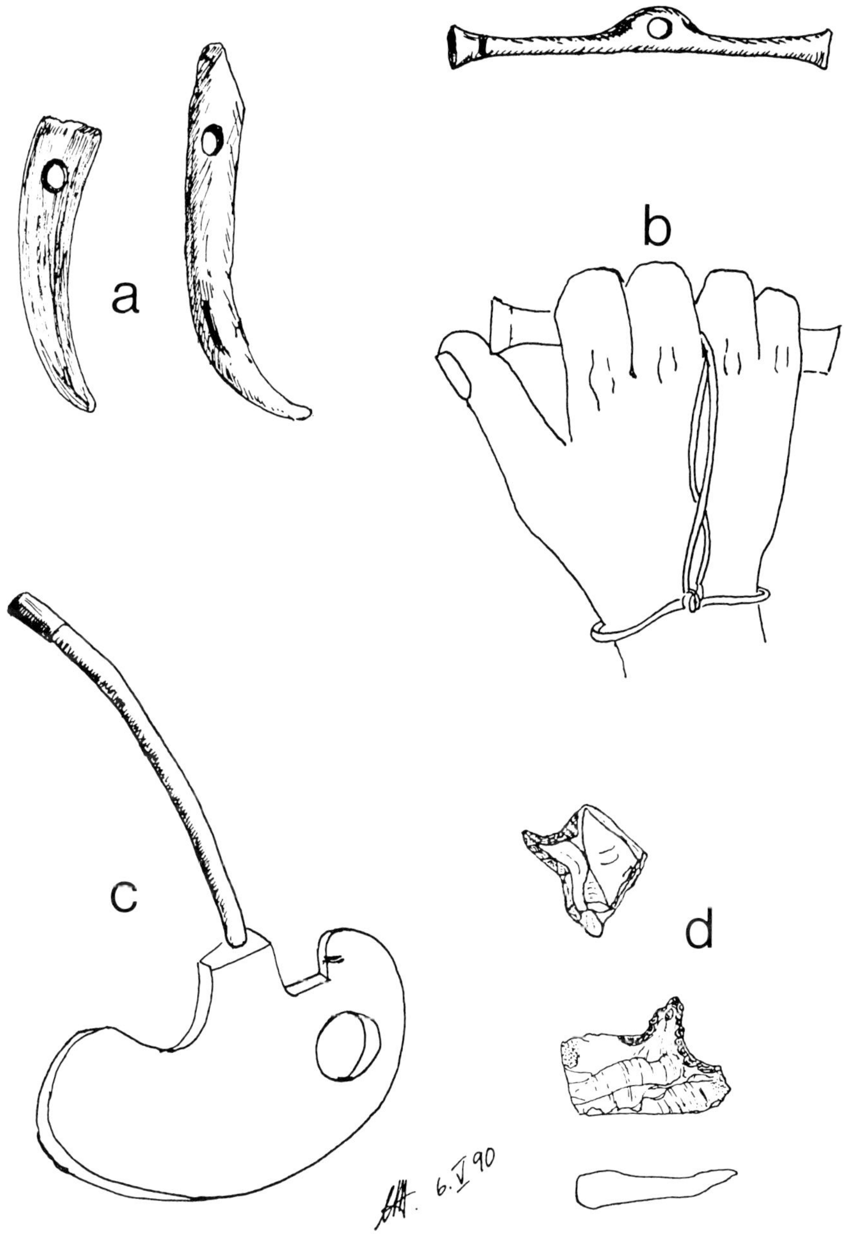

Figure 10: ANCILLARY EQUIPMENT.
(a) Toggles. (b) Pendant and suggested method of use.
(c) Disabled Archery Release Aid. (d) Scrapers.

The Mary Rose excavations produced a number of leather discs for holding 24 arrows together.

Release Aids for archery have been in use many thousands of years and are sometimes surprisingly similar to those 'developed' by today's archers. For example, **Linnaeus** wrote of the Laplanders holding the bow with their left hand and drawing it with their right by means of a cleft stick, ***bifidus ramus.*** The mittens worn by reindeer herders in Lapland are still split between the second and third finger in the right hand glove, to take the retaining cord of the cleft stick, although they will tell you they are made that way to allow easier access to sleigh reins.

Frobenius recorded that "Africans of the region also use a bent piece of wood around the palm of the hand. The bow string is hooked over the wooden strip above the base of the index finger and held in place by pressure of the adjacent thumb, which also assists in holding the arrow in place."

It was also noted in Papua/New Guinea that the natives there assisting the Australian forces had greatly increased the draw weight of their bows to shoot metal broadheads supplied to them, and in order to cope with this, were using boar's tusks as release aids in the same way.

A considerable number of boar's tusks and stag horns in the form of toggles have been recovered at various sites in Britain **(Fig.10(a)).** Were they purely for ornament, to hold cloaks together, or have we a previously unthought of use for them?

The bow pendants certainly would work successfully in the same role. A replica of the pendant recorded in the Barnack Grave-Group was made and shooting trials carried out extremely successfully **(Fig.10(b)).** Ian Kinnes records that the material used in constructing the pendant awaits analysis, but suggests it be bone, or perhaps sperm-whale or walrus ivory. Surface coloration is comparable with that of a patinated bronze, but the reason for this is again unknown. Is this staining from the presently unknown green staining substance used in early times to waterproof fletchings? It is pleasing to record that a very similar release aid is offered by Disabled Archery Co-ordination, Grand National Archery Society, for those children whose disability affects the opening of their fingers **(Fig.10(c)).**

In passing, Kinnes also records a bracer, although he calls it a wristguard, and states that as there are at either end a number of sheet gold caps, these would have prevented thonging or stitching.

May I submit that the bracer would have been bound the arm, the zig-zag caps would stop the binding slipping.

Scrapers must have obviously been used in the making of bows and arrows. Numbers of notched types recovered would have been ideal for arrow shaft preparation **(Fig.10(d)).** No in-depth study of bow and arrow making tools has really been done for Northern Europe. At Star Carr, Clark found some materials including rolls of birch bark which could have been used as adhesive. But note that birch bark has also been used as a close covering for composite bows. Heath and Chiara discovered not only stone scrapers but also bivalve shells with sharpened edges, a shell plane made by knocking a hole in the shell of the giant land snail, and a scraper made from the jaws complete with tusks, of a wild pig. They also found chisels made from rodents' teeth set in a handle.

Thumb Rings are a form of release aid peculiar to the Mongolian release, which will be dealt with here rather than under Technique. A bow released by means of a thumb ring has a sharper performance which greatly increases the bow's velocity. The method is far more difficult to master than any release normally used in Northern Europe, and for an archer to become proficient in this technique requires endless practice. The release is associated almost in its entirety with the composite bow. In the Mongolian release the bow string is pulled back by the thumb, whilst the tip of the forefinger is placed on the thumb nail for support **(Fig.11(a)).** It entails the wearing of a glove, leather guard or thumb ring. Practically all Asiatic races use this method: the Mongols, Scythians, Persians, Turks, Manchus, Tibetans, Indians, Chinese and Japanese. Certainly one could say that the archers employed during the Roman occupation of Britain were using thumb rings. Note that with the thumb ring, the arrow is placed on the right hand side of the bow, opposite to that met with any other form of release.

The illustration of the **Archer's paradox** is reversed, but otherwise the same considerations apply.

I have no knowledge of any thumb rings being identified from Roman sites in this country.

Hundreds of examples are known of thumb rings made in a variety of materials: silver, wood, porphyritic rock, marble, jasper, agate, alabaster, serpentine, quartz, porphry, jade, sandstone, etcetra. **(Fig.11(b))** shows a selection.

When not in use, the rings were sometimes carried in small containers suspended from a belt. These cases were made of wood,

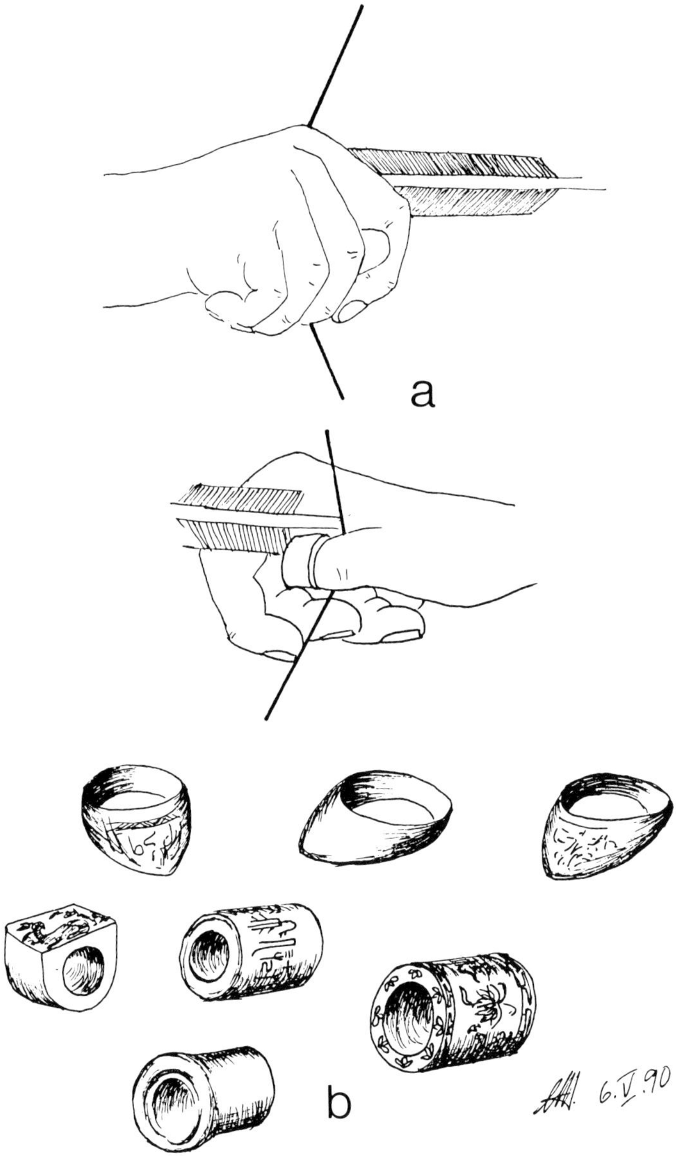

Figure 11: ANCILLARY EQUIPMENT
(a) Mongolian Release. (b) Selection of Thumb Rings.

horn, ivory, silk over paper and sometimes jade. The training in the use of the bow with the thumb ring began in early childhood, witness the finds of tiny rings, sometimes measuring less than half-an-inch internal diameter. Some of these rings would not be Thumb Rings used as release aids, but Thumb Guards used on the bow hand. Some of the Chinese rings have a little spur on the side of the ring, and if that ring is worn on the bow hand with the spur pressing against the bow handle, it provides a convenient arrow-shelf. Alternatively, if worn on the draw hand, those spurs touch the corner of the mouth at full draw, thus providing a positive check on the position of the arrow nock in relation to the eye.

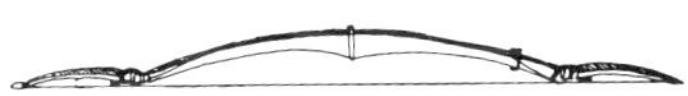

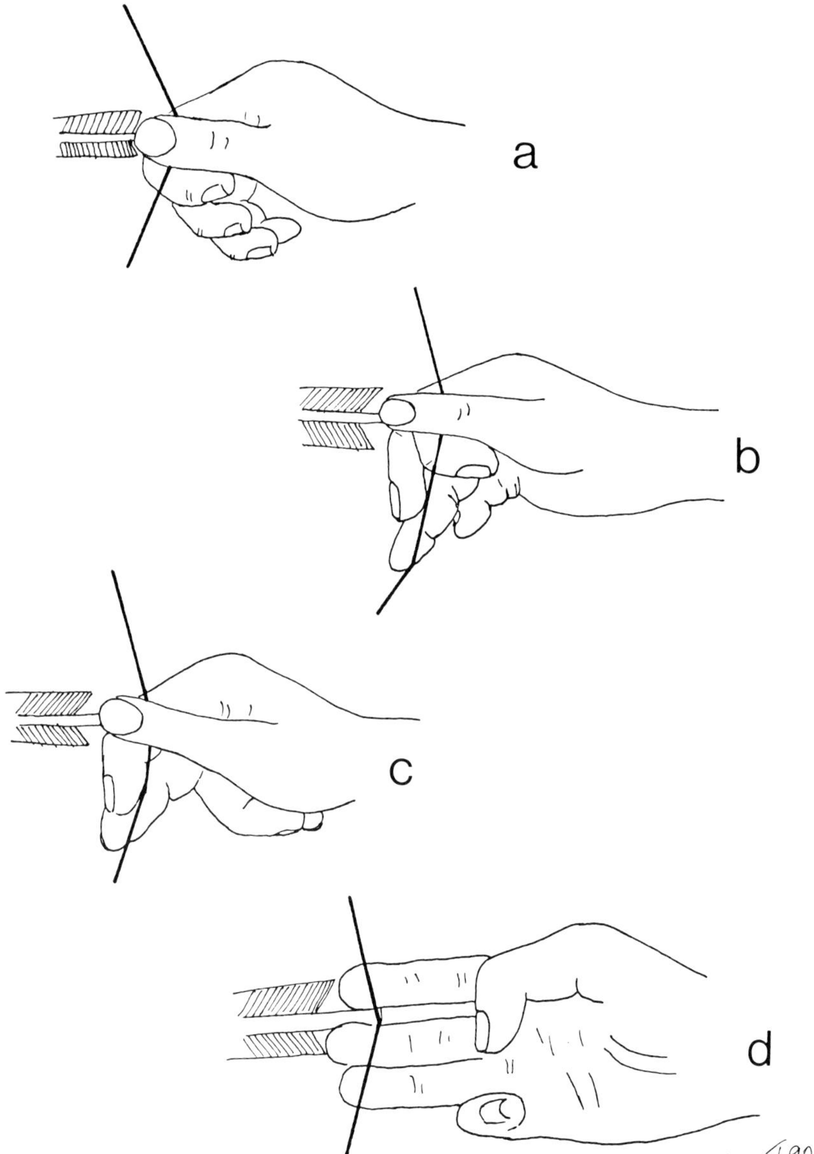

Figure 12: TECHNIQUES.
(a) Primary Release. (b) Secondary Release. (c) Tertiary Release.
(d) Mediterranean Release.

8

Techniques

A great number of books have bean written on the subject of archery technique. It is not the intention to repeat that material here, but to show how some techniques are recognisable by the arrows found in an archaeological context. The method adopted to place and hold an arrow to the string, and to draw and release it, is perhaps one of the most complex factors in the study of archery. There were five basic Release techniques identified by Morse, which will be briefly described to show the type of arrow used. One method, the Mongolian, has already been mentioned, as has a method using a release aid, not covered by Morse.

The Primary Release **(Fig. 12(a))** requires the butt end of the arrow to be held between the straightened thumb and the first and second joints of the bent forefinger. The string is pulled back by pulling on the arrow. It is only possible to use this method with weak bows. Some users of this method have the butt or nock of the arrow roughened (Andaman) or bulbous (Alaska).

The Secondary Release **(Fig. 12(b))** is a development of the Primary Release. Only the thumb and forefinger grasp the arrow, with the second and third fingers on the bow string assisting the draw.

The Tertiary Release **(Fig. 12(c))** is very similar, but recognised as a separate technique. The arrow is again grasped between the thumb and forefinger, but here the forefinger and the second are also on the string to assist in the drawing of the bow. The draw can be found modified, with two, three and four fingers being used to draw the string. Often this method requires the user to hold the bow hand thumb upright, and the arrow is shot between the bow handle and the upright thumb. This technique can be found in use in Papua/New Guinea, Surinam, Indonesia, Thailand and Burma.

None of the above require the arrow to be sufficiently nocked to fit on the bow string, and arrows can be found with no nocks, or only elementary nocks.

Both the Secondary and Tertiary Releases can be accurately described as 'assisted pinch-draws'.

The Mediterranean Release **(Fig. 12(d))** dates from the 20th Century BC according to Egyptian evidence. Here the arrow nock is so constructed as to fit fairly tightly on the bow string. The string is drawn by the tips of three fingers with the arrow lightly held like a cigarette, if held at all, between the first and second fingers. The little finger and thumb are not used. A variant of this release is often called the *Flemish Release*. This only employs the first and second fingers, and is very efficient if one's fingers are strong enough to stand the strain. It seems to be the method used in medieval times, hence the 'two fingered salute' used to show one's opponents that one's release fingers were complete.

Heath and Chiara do state however, that they had three observations of the Mediterranean Release being used by the ***Yanoama*** whose arrows have pronounced thickened butt ends, and that the notion that the use of the Primary Release is always associated with thickened butt ends, must be viewed with caution.

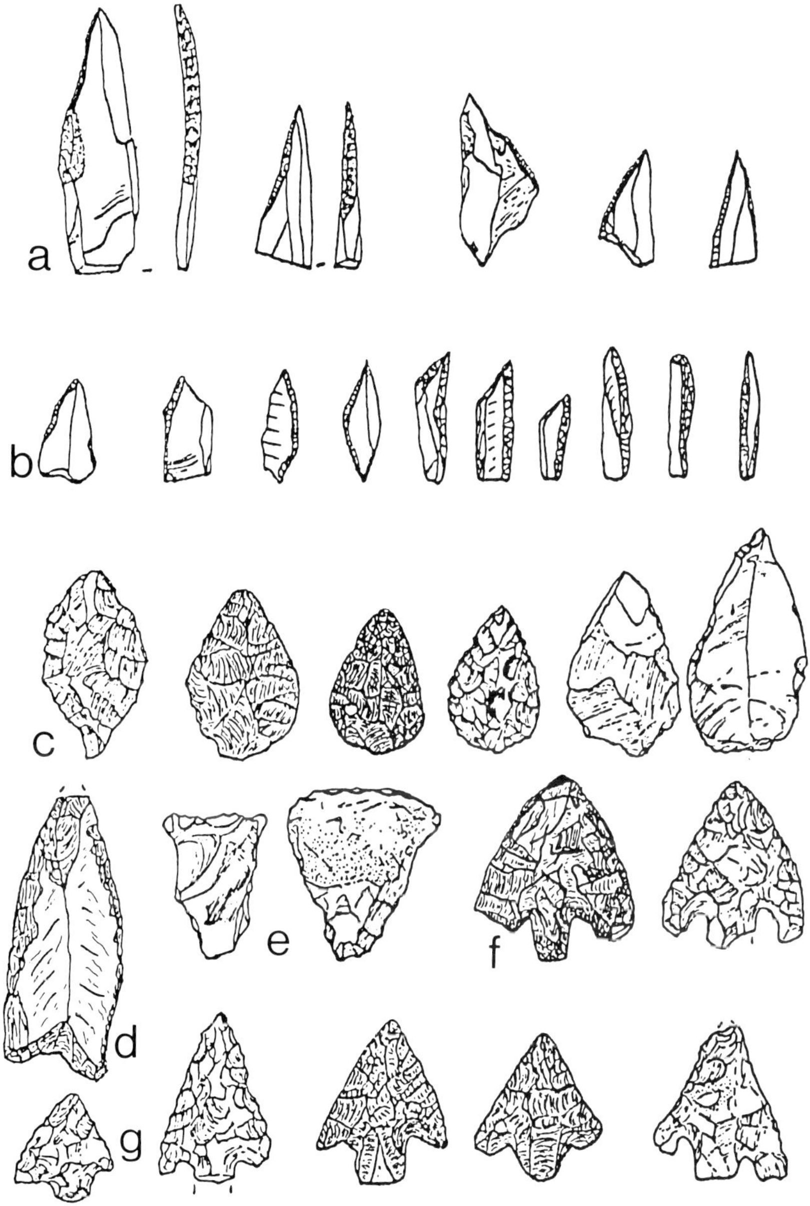

Figure 13: ARROWHEADS.

Flint projectile points from the Forest of Dean and Wye Valley.

(a) and (b) Mesolithic c.8,000 BC to 4,000BC. (c) Neolithic c.4,000 BC to c.2,000BC, Leaf shape. (d) A comparatively rare late Neolithic oblique. (e) Neolithic tranchet type. (f) and (g) Bronze Age barbed and tanged c.2,000 BC to 700 BC.

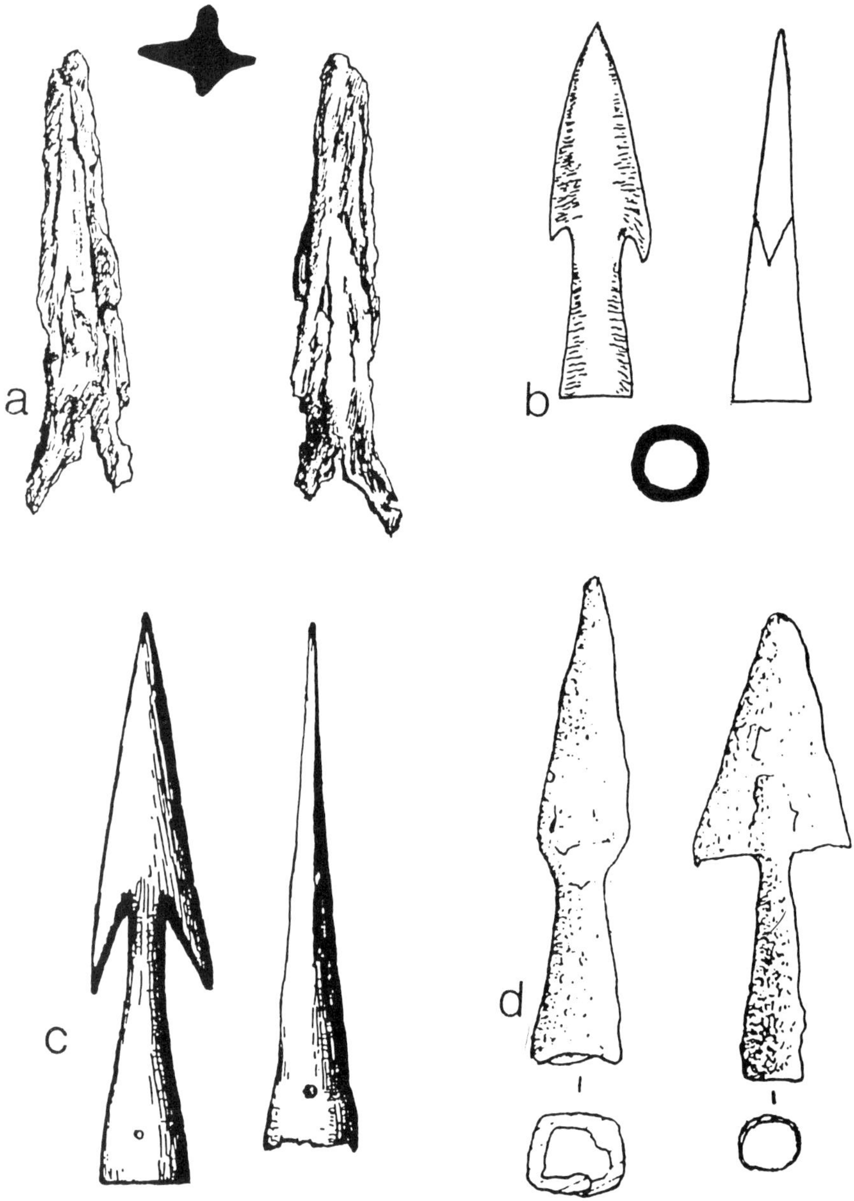

Figure 14: ARROWHEADS.
(a) A rare quad-lobed ballista head manufactured for the Roman military at ARICONIUM, Weston-on-Penyard, Herefordshire. (b) A 13th Century quarrel from EASTBACH, English Bicknor, Forest of Dean. (c) Two arrowheads from Dyserth. (d) Two from Laugharne Castle; b, c and d very probably manufactured at St. Briavels Castle 1200-1280 AD.

PLATE 1: *Society of Archer-Antiquaries member Alain Holt shooting a reproduction of a Mary Rose bow 1545 AD (Copyright). The arrows and clothing are also based on the Mary Rose finds. Photographs Roy C. Hingerford, ARPS. Thanks for permission to reproduce.*

PLATE 2 *Society of Archer-Antiquaries member with authentic Saudi Arabian equipment and costume*
Copyright & Photograph Roy C. Hungerford, ARPS, with thanks to both for permission to reproduce.

PLATE 3 *Bowyer Richard Galloway shooting a reproduction Egyptian self bow of acacia based on bows from Tut'ankhamun's tomb 1352 BC*
Copyright & Photograph Roy C. Hungerford, ARPS, with thanks to both for permission to reproduce.

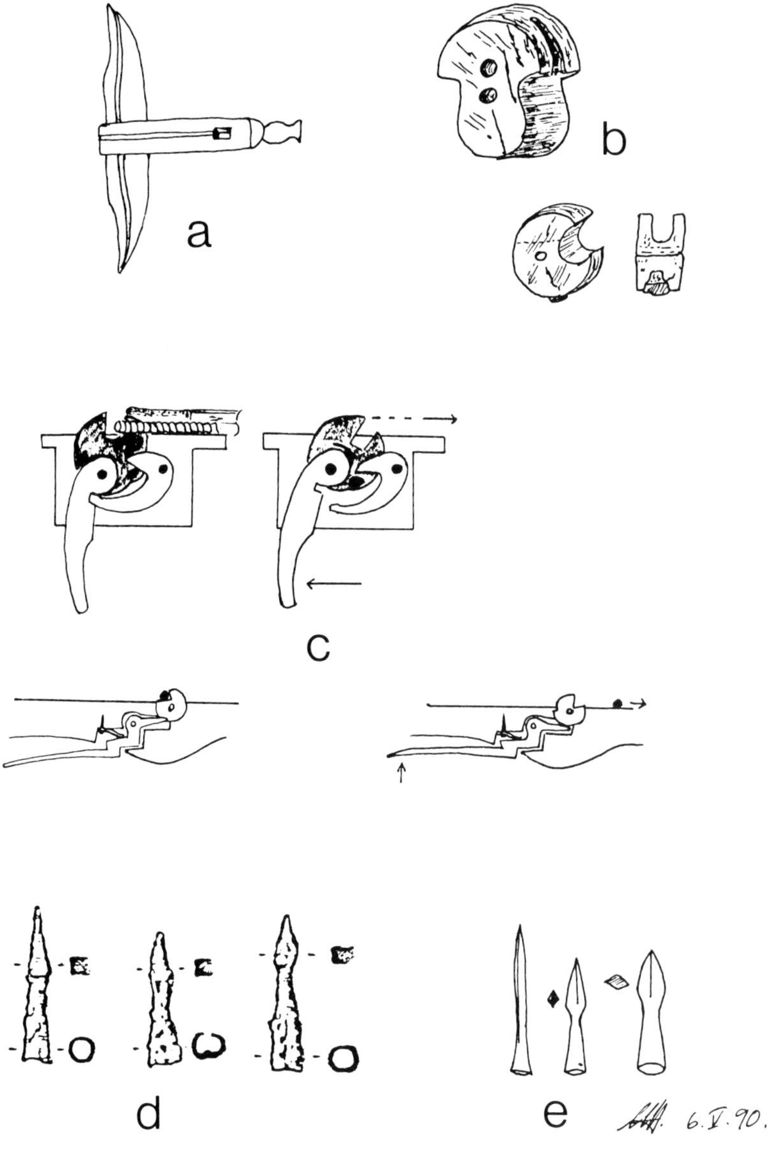

Figure 15: THE CROSSBOW.
(a) Gastrephretes. (b) The Nut. (c) Action of the Nut with alternative trigger.
(d) Roman bolt heads. (e) Medieval crossbow heads.

9

The Crossbow

The idea of mounting a bow on a stout crosspiece and providing a mechanical means of holding it at full draw, and releasing the string when required, is many centuries old. Generally the crossbow projects a missile with considerable force, especially over shorter distances. This energy although initially very great, is quickly expended, and thus the missiles have a penetration probably superior to the bow at short distances, being overtaken by the bow at longer distances. The crossbow can do greater damage but is often considered for static positions as it is a heavier and slower weapon to use.

Originating in Asia, the crossbow passed into Europe and there is ample evidence that not only large machines using the crossbow principle were used by the Romans, the ***manuballistaes, scorpio*** and the ***scorpio manualis,*** but also the Romans had a light portable crossbow, the ***gastrephretes,*** in use very early. **(Fig. 15(a))** is drawn from engravings on fragments of Roman tombstones in France. The mechanism probably incorporated the **nut,** featured in most crossbows from Europe. The nut is a skilfully shaped block of horn, antler or bone, with cut-outs in it, and although some improvements have been made, the basic design remains. At least two have been recovered from archaeological sites **(Fig.15(b)).** Originally reported as coming from Roman levels, there is now evidence that they are much later. However they are so distinctive that their outline is included here as an archaeological artefact readily recognisible.

The action is shown in **(Fig.15(c))** with the string pulled back, the nut revolved to latch and cock the trigger, and the release showing how the nut revolves back to its neutral position. An alternative trigger arrangement is also shown.

Traditionally Hengist and Horsa when they invaded Britain in AD 457 were supposed to have had the crossbow, as were the Norman invaders of 1066. The Domesday Book of 1085 mentions both lands held by the rent of a crossbow, and several ***arcuballistarii,*** captains of crossbowmen, holding lands as tenants-in-chief.

The crossbow became widespread in the 12th Century under the kings William II, Henry I and II, Richard I and John I. The Magna Carta has a passage: *"agree to banish from the kingdom, all the foreign knights, crossbowmen,"* whilst in 1139 crossbows were prohibited by Pope Innocent II as being: *"deathly and hateful to God and unfit to be used among Christians."* They could be used against the infidels. Richard Coeur de Lion was skilled in their use, and at the siege of Chaluz, near Limoges in France in 1199, he was wounded by a bolt which buried itself deep in his left shoulder. The story goes that the crossbowman, now a prisoner, was brought before the king, who pardoned him. Unfortunately the king died from his wound, and the prisoner was thereupon flayed alive.

By the reign of Henry III, the longbow was taking over although the crossbow was still considered superior. Two of my recent papers tell the story of John Malemort, King's Quarreller at St. Briavels Castle from 1223 to 1283, and the production of over a million quarrels for crossbows. There was one short period of crossbow bolt production in the early 14th Century, but from that date greater emphasis was placed on the longbow. Even so, it was the custom to place crossbowmen as watchmen in the castles. It is hoped that eventually it will be possible to mount a thorough excavation of the 'Quarrel Fields' site near St. Briavels Castle, with a view to obtaining more information on the manufacturing processes.

A primitive crossbow was identified by Alm excavated from a site at Lillohus, Kristianstad, Sweden, and an early 13th Century crossbow almost complete is in the Schweizeriches, Zurich. There are considerable numbers of later crossbows held by museums, ancient homes and in private collections. This must not be taken to prove that the crossbow outnumbered the longbow.

The crossbow was the ***lord's*** property and held by him in his armoury whilst the longbow was the ***commoner's*** weapon and usually ended its days in the cottage, smoke blackened by the chimney breast. An old longbow looks just like an old bent stick, whilst anyone can easily recognise a crossbow. Thus longbows were rarely preserved, and apart from the considerable number recovered from the Mary Rose, the others can be counted on the fingers of one hand.

There are numbers of crossbows in ethnographical collections from all over the world, from the huge whaling crossbows of Norway and Iceland, to small hand pistol types from Malaya. Some have a much simpler trigger mechanism. The stock is split like an old fashioned clothes peg, the string pulled back to a notch and held. To release, the two split ends of the stock are closed. Strangely, there are two widely separated places where crossbows modelled on those carried by Portuguese travellers of the medieval period can be found. The ***Yoruba*** of South-Western Nigeria copied it with all the fittings in bronze instead of iron, whilst the same crossbow turns up in ***Cochin,*** an Indian state on the Malabar coast, but this time all the fittings are in wood.

The projectile shot from a crossbow can be called an **arrow,** a **bolt,** or a **quarrel.** There do not seem to be any rules on this usage, so I adopt the differentiation as used by today's users of the crossbow. If it is as long, or longer, than the draw of the crossbow, it is an arrow. If it is shorter than the draw of the crossbow, it is a bolt. Quarrel is a 13th Century term, probably from the old French ***quarreau,*** modern French ***carreau,*** meaning in effect four-sided, square or diamond shaped. These heads are a common shape for early medieval crossbow shafts.

Generally one would expect the heads to be socketed unless there is extra metal left on the head to stop it being rammed back into the shaft when tanged. The Durden Collection has one of the largest groups of catapult bolt heads from any one Roman site. A great proportion are 6.8 to 7.0 cms long, with others of up to 8.1 cms. **(Fig.15(d))** illustrates a number of these.

The London Museum catalogue illustrates arrow and bolt heads of the medieval period. Types 7, 8 and 9 are more likely to be crossbow heads, with 8 and 9 termed at the time 'quarrels.' **(Fig.15(e))** shows a selection of the period.

The ancillary equipment of the crossbowmen can be identified. Often the bow (or **prod** as it is termed by the Americans) of the crossbow is too strong to be pulled back by hand, and various mechanical means have to be utilised. These can range from the belt and claw, windlass, cranequin, and 'goat's foot' lever. The belt and claw method used the belt around the user's waist with the claw attached to it. The crossbow string was hooked on the claw, and by using a stirrup fitted in front of the bow, the user pressed down with one foot to cock the crossbow.

This was the **one-foot** crossbow of medieval records. A system of pulleys and ropes comprised the windlass for spanning the heavy siege crossbows. One man could cock and prepare for action but the tackle is cumbersome and time consuming. Many of these windlasses can be seen hung up on display - often the ropes are tangled together and it is difficult to see the action. The cranequin similarly copes with heavy weight crossbows. By turning a crank, a pinion engages a ratchet which draws back a double hook over the string. The steel bows which appeared by the end of the 14th Century all required this mechanical assistance. The goat's foot lever is a simpler device, still in use with crossbows today. The gaffle is a similar instrument. Some crossbows have an integral bending-lever built in. All three depend on the leverage principle to cock the crossbow.

The military crossbowman usually sheltered behind his pavise or shield, especially when his back was bent and unprotected whilst he cocked and loaded the crossbow. Many had a paviser, a man to carry and operate the shield for them. These highly ornate pavises can often be found.

10

Ethnographic Evidence

Whilst there are few books describing archery equipment in an archaeological context, there appear to be a great number on anthropology, ethnology and ethnography with many references to archery equipment. I use the word, ethnography, in the old sense: the study of equipment and material belongings of native races. Many modern dictionaries seem to have dropped the word - putting both culture and equipment under the one heading - ethnology.

Generally bows can be divided into four broad types. The map shows the distribution of (a) bows of self wood, including handle-reinforced types, longbows and laminated types; (b) the Eskimo type with loose sinew backings; (c) the Asiatic composite, fully close covered and (d) the range of Red Indian bows with their mixture of backed bows, of horn and sinew, and of simple self wood bows. Although a number of Asiatic composite bows are found loose sinew backed, for simplicity it is easier to term them Eskimo type. There are minor deviations from the boundaries shown; they are a basic device to illustrate spheres of influence.

Fast disappearing is the hunter-gatherer way of life. One cannot draw a map and say "Here are Hunter-Gatherers." Accordingly the map is also marked with just twelve groups who were active in the last two hundred years, where there is a fair amount of documentary evidence. To these must be added the ***Veddahs*** of Sri Lanka, the ***Andamanese*** of the Andaman Islands, the ***Bhutan*** of the Himalayas and the ***Ainu*** of Hokkaido, Northern Japan. There have been some extremely good studies of these people, but every time a researcher visits them, it is another step nearer their complete extinction. One cannot help but remember the substantial change in Papuan archery towards the end of World War Two. In an all-out effort to rid the islands of isolated Japanese troops, the Australians recruited large numbers of natives. They provided them with metal broadheads. These proved too heavy

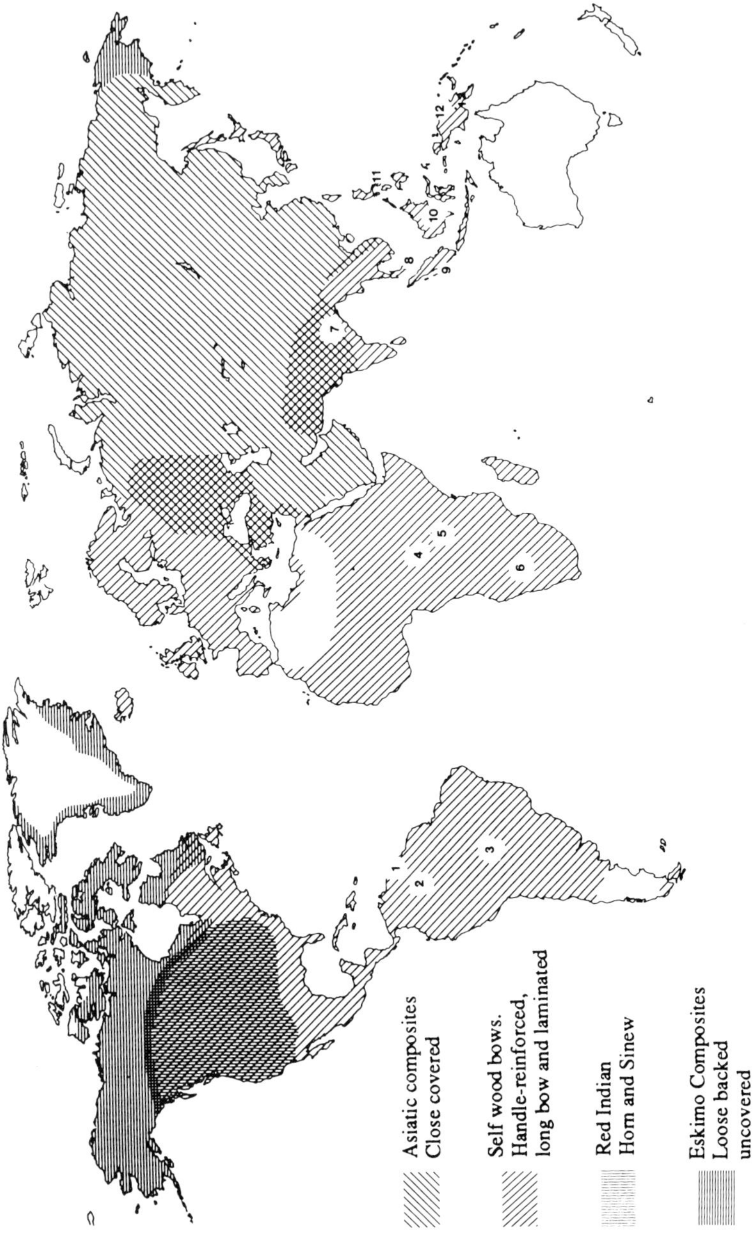

RECENT HUNTER-GATHERERS: These were surviving up to the last two hundred years. 1, Xinguan. 2, Shiriana. 3, Bororo. 4, Negrillo. 5, Hadza. 6, San. 7, Birhor. 8, Semang. 9, Sumatran. 10, Punan. 11, Tasaday. 12, Papuan.

for the native bows, so new heavier bows were made. These new bows were too heavy to pull with the fingers, so they used the boar's tusks they wore as ornaments as a release aid. Thus we had a change from a group using mainly hardwood tipped arrows with the occasional use of bone and shell, and little knowledge of stone or metal, using equipment completely foreign to them.

In the past, one had the ***Kazuk, Kirghiz*** and ***Kalmuch*** horse breeders of Central Asia, all using the loose sinew backed composite, although one would be lucky to find one now. In Siberia, the reindeer hunters of the Northern Tungus used a laminated wood bow - probably of the type recently found in Lapland - the belly timber dovetailed into the back timber, not glued, just held under tension by the fit. Alongside these people, the ***Yukaghir*** had the loose backed composite. In British Columbia, the ***Nootka*** and ***Kwakuth*** had good solid longbows of yew, more like early Scandinavian models. In Tierra del Fuego, the ***Yahgan*** had similar bows whilst the ***Ona*** had one that was multi-faceted in cross section. The ***Ainu*** had a very stiff self bow shooting only 16-inch arrows, and the ***Andaman Islands*** bow has a complicated S shape, unknown anywhere else.

The Australian Aborigines did not have the bow; those few found in the north are undoubted imports from Papua/New Guinea. The ***Masai*** cattle breeders of East Africa keep a bow purely for blood letting. A leather thong is tightly strapped around a bullock's neck causing a large vein to swell up. It is then pierced with a special arrow with a wide transverse blade, hollowed to carry the blood to a container. Poison is used by the ***San*** of the Kalahari from the bodies of dried grubs; the ***Semang*** go up into the highlands to collect the sap from the upas tree, whilst most of the Brazilian Indians use curare.

One can highly recommend the work of Heath and Chiara on their study of Brazilian Indian Archery, one of the few recent publications. The updated second edition of Native American Bows is a joy with its appendix on the making of horn bows. Otherwise most publications are many years old. Cranstone has a good ethnography on Melanesia from 1960, but apart from small booklets on the ***Hadza*** and ***San*** produced by the Museum of Mankind, one has to go back to Mainguard or Lommel, both published in the 1930's for African archery. Regrettably neither the Shire Ethnography series or Egyptology series have yet covered any archery equipment. Many Journals of the Society of Archer-Antiquaries contain good articles on native archery, but one must appreciate that they are mainly culled from earlier publications and not reports of recent visits.

NOTES

Bibliography

ALLCHIN,B. 1966 — The Stone Tipped Arrow.

ALM,J. 1946 — Europeiska Armborst, *Vaaben-Historiske Aarbager,* Vol. Vb.

ANDERSEN,S.H. 1978 — An 8000 Year Old Arrow from Vendsyssel, Northern Jutland, *Acta Arch. Vol. 49.*

BECKER,C.J. 1945 — En 8000 Arig stenalderboplads in Holmegaards Mose, *Nationmuseets Arbejdsmark, 1945.*

BROWN,F.E. 1937 — A Recently Discovered Compound Bow, *Anales de l'institut Kondakov, Vol. 9.*

CLARK,J.G.D. — Derivative forms of the *petit tranchet* in Britain.
1934 — Arch. Jnl. 91.
1936 — The Mesolithic Settlement of Northern Europe.
1938 — The Reindeer Hunting Tribes of Northern Europe. Antiq. 1938.
1963 — Neolithic bows from Somerset, England and the prehistory of archery in. North-Western Europe. PPS. 29.
1971 — (with Walker, Godwin, Frazer and King) Excavations at Star Carr, an Early Mesolithic Site at Seamer, near Scarborough, Yorkshire.
1975 — The Earlier Stone Age Settlement of Scandinavia.

CRANSTONE,B.A.L. 1960 — Melanesia, A Short Ethnography.

CREDLAND,A.G. 1975 — The Pellet Bow in Europe and the East. Soc. Arch-Ant. Jnl. Vol. 18.

DAVIES,J.L. 1977 — Roman Arrowheads from DINORBEN and the *Sagittarii* of the Roman Army, Britannia Vol. 8.

DILLON,Viscount. — Arms and Armour at Westminster, the Tower and Greenwich, 1547, Archaeologia Vol. 51.

EMBLETON,R. and GRAHAM,F. 1984 — HADRIAN'S WALL in the days of the Romans.

EMERY, W. B. 1948 — Nubian Treasure.

EVANS,J. 1897 — The Ancient Stone Implements, Weapons and Ornaments of Gt. Britain.

FREY,G.J. 1990 — Archery Release Aids: the evolution and revolution. Soc. Arch-Ant. Jnl. Vol.33

GLOVER,W. 1979 — A Prehistoric Bow Fragment from Drumwhinny Bog, Kesh, Co. Fermanagh, PPS. 45.

GODWIN,H. 1967 — The Ancient Cultivation of Hemp, Ant. Vol. XLI.

GRAHAM-CAMPBELL,J. 1980 — Viking Artefacts: A select catalogue, Bows and Arrows.

GREEN,S. 1980 — The Flint Arrowheads of the British Isles.

HAMILTON,T.M. 1982 — Native American Bows, Missouri Archaeological Society, Special Pubs.No.5.

HEATH,E.G. and CHIARA,V. 1977 — Brazilian Indian Archery.

HENKEN,Dr.H.O'N. 1935 — Jnl R.S. Antiq. Ireland Vol. 5.

JACKSON,G.E. 1988 — The Compound Bow - A Short History, Soc. Arch-Ant. Jnl. Vol. 31.

KOSKO,A. and KLOCHKO,V.I. 1987 — A Late Neolithic Composite Bow. Soc. Arch-Ant. Jnl. Vol. 30.

KOZLOWSKI,S.K. 1973 — The Mesolithic in Europe. 1973.

LAIRD,R.D. 1984 — How to Make and Use the Atlati: The Ancient Weapon of the Ice Age Hunters, Saratoga Museum Papers No. 1.

LITVINSKI,B.A. 1966 — The composite Bow in Ancient Central Asia, *Sovietskaya Arcbeolglya*.

LOMMEL,B. 1932 — Morphology of the African Bow-Weapon, by Frobenius. Translated by Lommel.

LONDON MUSEUM 1954 — Medieval Catalogue, Arrowheads.

McLEOD,W. 1970 — Composite Bows from the Tomb of Tut'ankhamun. Tut'ankhamun Tomb Series No. 3.

MAINGUARD,L.F. 1932 — History and Distribution of the Bow and Arrow in South Africa, S. Afric. Jnl. of Science, Vol. XXIX.

MALMER,M. 1966 — Die Mikrolithen in dem Pfeil-Fund von Loshult, *Meddelanden fran Lunds Universitets Historiska*.

MANNING,W.H. 1985 — Catalogue of Romano-British Tools, Fittings and Weapons in the British Museum.

MEDVEV,A.F. 1966 — Missile Hand Weapons: Bows and Arrows, Crossbows of the VII - XIV Centuries. Moscow Foreign Language.

MINTY,R.G.P. 1870 — A Horn Bow from the Cambridgeshire Fens. Antiq.

MORSE,E.S. 1885 — Ancient and Modern Methods of Arrow Release, Essex Institute Bulletin, Vol. XVII.
1922 — Additional Notes on Arrow Release, Peabody Museum.

NEADE,W. 1625 — The Double-Armed Man.

MUNSTER. 1958 — North Munster Arch. Jnl. Vol. VIII, Desmond Castle.

OKLADNIKOV,A.P. 1950 — Neolit i bronzovyl vek Pribaikalia, "Materialy i issledeovani-ja po archeologii SSSR". Moscow.

PETERSSON,M. 1951 — Mikrolithen als Pfeilspitzen Ein Fund aus dem Lilla Loshult-Moor, Ksp, Loshult, Skane., *Meddelanden fran Lunds Universitets Historiska Museum*.

PIGGOTT,S. 1971 — 'Beaker Bows: A Suggestion', PPS XXXVII.

PRATT,Prof.P.L. and HARDY,R. 1975 — "The Arrow Found in Westminster Abbey in 1878," Soc. Arch-Ant. Jnl. Vol. 18.

RAUSING,G.	The Bow: Some notes on its origin and development.
1967	Lund.
RULE,M.	The Mary Rose.
1982	
SMITH,J.E.	*Lachesis Lapponica,* or a Tour in Lapland. Translation of Linnaeis
1811	Journal.
SWITSUR,R.	A Longbow from Denny.
1974	Antiq. Vol. 48, No. 189.
TROELS-SMITH,J.	En Elmetraes-Bue fra Aamosen og andra traesager fra tidlig-
1959	neolitiske tid, *Aarboger for Nordisk Oldkyndished og Historie.*
1961	Et pileskaft fra tidlig maglemosetid, *Aarboger for Nordisk Oldkyndished og Historie.*
WILKE,P.J.	"Bow Staves Harvested from Juniper Trees by Indians of Nevada,"
1988	Jnl. California and Great Basin Anthro. Vol. 10, No. 1.
WEBB,A. with GORDON.H.	The Hedgeley Moor Bow at Alnick Castle.
1972	Soc. Arch-Ant. Jnl. Vol. 15.
with GORDON,H.	The Flodden Bow at Archers' Hall, Edinburgh.
1974a	Soc. Arch-Ant .Jnl. Vol. 17.
with GORDON.H.	The Mary Rose Bows at the Tower of London.
1974b	Soc. Arch-Ant .Jnl. Vol. 17.
with GORDON.H.	Prehistoric Bows of Britain.
1976	Soc. Arch-Ant .Jnl. Vol. 19.
with GORDON.H.	Prehistoric Bows of Britain.
1978	Soc. Arch-Ant .Jnl. Vol. 21.
	Prehistoric Bows in Ireland.
1980	Soc. Arch-Ant .Jnl. Vol. 23.
	"How did the bow develop?".
1981	Pop. Arch. Dec. 1981.
	The So-called Bow Puller,
1982	Pop. Arch. Mar. 1982.
	"Some Questions Archer-Antiquarians would like to put to Archaeologists".
1984	Pop. Arch. Enclosure, May. 1984.
	John Malemort - King's Quarreller, Part.1.
1988	Soc. Arch-Ant .Jnl. Vol. 31.
	John Malemort - King's Quarreller, Part 2.
1989	Soc. Arch-Ant .Jnl. Vol. 32.
	Prehistoric Archery - Some Considerations.
1989	Dean Archaeology No. 2.
	Roman Use of the Bow and Crossbow.
1990	Dean Archeology, No. 3.

NOTES

Appendix 1

*Prehistoric archery can be the key to a door unlocking a vast amount of information for archaeology. The raw materials used in making the artefacts - locally produced, or obtained by trade or barter? The shape, style, method of manufacture - who made them, what purpose did they serve? This key, however, needs two pairs of hands to operate it - one the archaeologist, the other the archer. The archaeologists may well lack the skills to construct replicas of the equipment and use it effectively. The archer may have the skills, but may lack the knowledge of prehistory to be able to ask tbe **right** questions.*

The closest co-operation between the two is tbe way ahead.

BRITISH LONG-BOW SOCIETY

This Society exists to serve archers wishing to shoot the traditional long-bow under the old shooting rules. Membership gives access to factual and historical information with questions answered through the medium of a large Collection of antique equipment, and an extensive library. The associated Craft Guild of Traditional Bowyers & Fletchers (bow and arrow makers) provides a point of contact for archer-archaeologists seeking replica bows.

Contact:- Hugh Soar, Hon. Secretary
65, Chiltern Close, Warmley, BRISTOL, BS15 5UL

GRAND NATIONAL ARCHERY SOCIETY

This is the controlling body for archery in Great Britain.

Contact:- The Grand National Archery Society, 7th Street, National Agricultural Centre, Stoneleigh, KENILWORTH, Warks, CV8 2LG

SIMON ARCHERY COLLECTION

The Simon Archery Collection is housed in two Simon Archery Rooms adjacent to The Manchester Museum. It consists of archery material from all over the world, and providing prior arrangements are made with the Hon. Keeper, anybody is welcome to visit and study. The Simon Archery Foundation was formed to administer a Trust endowed by Erna Simon in 1970, and has as its object the collection of archive material and to act as a repository for material relating to the development of archery. The Foundation also publishes important works of Archery.

Contact:- Hon. Keeper, Simon Archery Collection, Mrs. A. Wendy Hodkinson,
The Manchester Museum, The University, MANCHESTER, M13 9PL

SOCIETY OF ARCHER-ANTIQUARIES

Formed for those interested in the history and development of the bow, it is now an international learned society. It publishes an annual Journal and a newsletter, *Arrowhead*. It has archival material, books and collections of equipment.

Contact:- Arrowhead Editor, Alf Webb, 5, Park Court, Bathurst Park Road,
LYDNEY, Glos., GL15 5HG

Index

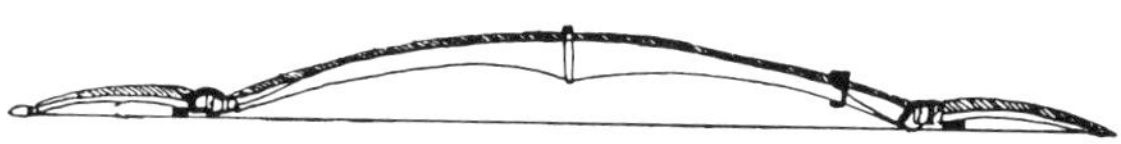

"The Glade" (jointly with Dean Archaeology Group) is the publisher of "Archaeology of Archery" and enquiries concerning it should be addressed to:

Ted Bradford,
62 Hook Rise North,
Tolworth, Surrey, KT6 7JY, England.